Gratitude and Grace

Joel

13 October 2009

The Writings of Michael Mayne

Joel W. Huffstetler

University Press of America,® Inc.
Lanham · Boulder · New York · Toronto · Plymouth, UK

Copyright © 2009 by
University Press of America,® Inc.
4501 Forbes Boulevard
Suite 200
Lanham, Maryland 20706
UPA Acquisitions Department (301) 459-3366

Estover Road
Plymouth PL6 7PY
United Kingdom

Library of Congress Control Number: 2009930770
ISBN-13: 978-0-7618-4750-2 (paperback : alk. paper)
ISBN-10: 0-7618-4750-2 (paperback : alk. paper)
eISBN-13: 978-0-7618-4751-9
eISBN-10: 0-7618-4751-0

♾™ The paper used in this publication meets the minimum
requirements of American National Standard for Information
Sciences—Permanence of Paper for Printed Library Materials,
ANSI Z39.48-1992

To
Alison Mayne

TABLE OF CONTENTS

FOREWORD

In 1984 I was working as a speech therapist at a big hospital in Cambridge, England. I regularly saw a thin, dark-haired and elegant priest walking the long corridors; he reminded me a little of Fred Astaire, and I was drawn to the intelligence and sensitivity of his face. I had been brought up as a Christian but was at that time troubled by a myriad questions of faith, and had long wanted to be able to ask *any* question of an open and thoughtful practical theologian. I found out his name – Michael Mayne – and that he was the vicar of the Cambridge University Church – Great St. Mary's. Placing my courage onto pen and paper, I wrote to him, asking if we might meet for me to explore some problems and questions. He responded at once – 'Dear Christina, what you ask is very simple.' This led to regular meetings of what I now know can be termed 'pastoral counselling'; at that time I simply knew that they offered me a rich well of listening, wisdom and spiritual discussion.

When these ended, Michael invited me to have lunch at the vicarage and I met his wife, Alison, along with their teenage son Mark and daughter Sarah. The house was full of warmth and light, and we all played with the six puppies that had recently been born to their much-loved golden retriever. Soon afterwards, Michael developed the myalgic encephalitis (ME) – so eloquently described in *A Year Lost and Found*. One of his many uncomfortable symptoms was a sensation that he did not have enough breath, and he asked me to show him some breathing exercises. I was glad to be able to give him something after all he had given me, and it enabled our professional relationship to develop into a more equal friendship.

I started to attend the services and talks at Great St. Mary's, and felt its loss when I then had to move to London. Wanting to find a church in my new home area, Michael wrote me an informative but very funny kind of informal 'Guide to Good Churches of North London'. Something that is perhaps needed in many places! Sadly none were like that fine Cambridge church, and none of the preachers were like Michael – but then how could they be?

Gratitude and Grace brings to life Michael's writing. He wrote as he spoke as he was – compassionate, sensitive, thoughtful, humorous and luminously intelligent. These qualities infused his preaching, and as Joel Huffstetler makes so clear, his very wide reading and his relish for the power and poetry of words were a major part of his tool-kit. Parallel with his writing skills was the power of his speaking. Michael was a *great* speaker. My work is now with the spoken voice, in both public speakers and voice disorders. Michael had a truly beautiful voice – deep, warmly resonant and with a delicate balance of dark and light qualities. As we will read, he had considered acting and would almost certainly have been a success; he had a brilliant imagination, intuitive verbal timing, emotional sensitivity, quick wit and deft physical energy – indeed he gave the impression he could probably even dance like Fred Astaire at times! He brought those skills – without the actor's essential need to dissemble of course – into his ministry.

Over the years my friendship with Michael and Alison grew closer and deeper. They supported me through a change of career, the ups and downs of a single woman in London and the early days of my relationship with Mark, who became my husband. In fact in 1988, the only two people present at the quietly sacred blessing ceremony of our marriage, in the 13th century St. Faith's chapel of Westminster Abbey, were Michael and Alison.

Michael's ten years as administrative and pastoral head of the great church of Westminster Abbey were very rich. He loved the fabric and history of that vast ancient building, and took great pleasure in showing round small groups of dinner guests after the Abbey had been closed to the public for the night. Those of us lucky enough to tread softly around its enormous cool emptiness will never forget those quiet special tours of stone, space, tombs and memorials. Although one of the most senior churchmen in the UK, regularly mixing with royalty and politicians, Michael never lost his connection to the ordinary man and woman of his congregation and continued to see people for individual counselling.

During a sabbatical from his heavy duties, Michael went to write in the Swiss mountains and much of *This Sunrise of Wonder: Letters to my grandchildren* was drafted there. Alison describes how there was barely room for their cases as the mass of books took up most of the room in the car; certainly the resulting book bubbles and fizzes with illuminating references.

Michael *adored* books; he collected them, showed them, quoted from them, shared them and rarely got rid of any. The construction of bookcases, and the ordering of books were core to the home-making process as he and Alison began their retirement in the country town of Salisbury, about 70 miles from London. He wrote his three next books in his quiet book-lined attic study there, with a long view of the fine spire of Salisbury Cathedral. A year after his death, Alison, with all her gentleness and generosity, offered that room to me as a place for my own book writing. I sat for four weeks at Michael's desk, frequently struggling with what T. S. Eliot described as 'the intolerable wrestle with words and meanings', but comforted by a strong sense of Michael's presence in that quiet place.

Pray, Love, Remember was the first of his own books to be written there, and the book launch celebrations for this, and for the following *Learning to Dance*, were held in the medieval Jerusalem Chamber at the Abbey, by kind permission of his successor Dean. In that same chamber, Michael had instituted the series of 'Personal Choice' evenings, where successful actors came to read their own choice of prose and poetry to an invited audience who gave donations to organisations that supported those living with HIV/AIDS. Michael asked me to join him for the final evening of the events to mark his retirement, when he and I read our own favourite choices to guests who came to acknowledge and say good-bye to him. As usual his selection was wonderfully eclectic and included A. A. Milne, Emily Dickinson, Stevie Smith, Edwin Muir, Eilean Ni Chuilleanain, his beloved George Herbert and an anonymous humorous Cockney dialect poem called 'Dahn the Plug'ole'.

I enjoyed seeing the rich new life that Michael and Alison built in Salisbury, and visited when I could. For several years we shared Christmas Eves when they came over to my hometown where Sarah and her family lived for a while, when her husband Dan was curate at a local church. We would also sometimes meet to go to see an excellent local acting company, for they both continued to be passionate about good theatre. From Salisbury it is only an hour to the Dorset coast where my family have a little caravan in a tiny field on the edge of the sea. Michael loved the sea and would plunge into it in all kinds of weather and wild water. In our visitors' book is a little watercolour painting of a small figure swimming in a dark sea lit by moonlight. It was painted by Michael in 2003, and above it he wrote:

A windy but invigorating three days. Lots of reading, walking the cliffs amongst the scabious, campions and knapweed, refreshment at the pub and swimming in a choppy sea. But best of all, a magical evening when the sky cleared and the wind suddenly dropped so that the sea became still as glass, and after a rich sunset a three-quarters moon lit a trail on the water which drew me into the sea close to midnight. Unforgettable!

And then one day I came home to find a simple message from Michael on my answer phone, asking me to ring. There was something in his voice that made me anxious, and when we spoke he told me of his diagnosis of cancer. *The Enduring Melody* describes the process of that disease and its treatment; it was a long and grueling journey for him and for his most loving family. Yet he was able to write about it with such light, as if a composer whose final work contains all the exuberance, harmony and silence of a lifetime.

The second to last time I saw Michael was the party to celebrate that book. It was held in Salisbury just three weeks before his death; Michael was extremely frail and he and the family decided that I would be a kind of 'minder' – complete with badge – to protect him from having to struggle to speak to all the many guests. In the event, I was utterly redundant. Michael shone from his wheel chair, talking and laughing with everyone there and finding an energy that carried him through until well into the next day.

The book you are about to read beautifully describes, reflects upon and illuminates Michael's books, and the quality of his writing. In *Pray, Love, Remember*, he writes of the poets and novelists celebrated in Westminster Abbey's Poets' Corner, and says: 'they come closer than most of us in capturing in words or sounds the mystery of a world in which matter is the bearer of spirit.' So it was with you Michael. So it was with you.

Christina Shewell
Bristol, England

PREFACE

In 1996, Frederick Buechner was the keynote speaker for the Bowen Lectures series at Kanuga Conference Center in North Carolina. Other participants in the conference included Sam Lloyd and my dear friend, George Connor, who served as the conference's facilitator. Several years after the conference, George, knowing my considerable admiration for Buechner's writings, very kindly offered me access to cassette tapes of the Bowen Lectures before he donated his copies thereof to the library of St. Paul's Episcopal Church, Chattanooga, Tennessee, where he was a communicant and where I was then serving as a member of the pastoral staff. In handing me the package containing the cassettes, George noted, "*You* will also appreciate the meditations by the conference's chaplain, Michael Mayne." My friend was right.

Such was my appreciation of Mayne's contributions to the lectures that I immediately ordered each of his (then) four major books from *amazon.co.uk.*, as they were, at that time, unavailable from any well-known retail outlet in the United States. My subsequent reading of each of the books led to a series of four classes at St. Paul's in which each of the works was studied in detail. During my tenure as Rector of St. Luke's Episcopal Church in Cleveland, Tennessee, Mayne's fifth major work was published, and for the Lenten series of 2008, I offered reviews of each of the books on five successive Wednesday evenings.

The responses of class attendees over the years have mirrored my own initial response to Mayne's writings: "Why have I not heard of this person?" and "Why aren't his books more widely read?" In North America Mayne is, indeed, a largely unknown figure. Such is not the case, however, in the United Kingdom, where his books have found a significant audience. Having served as Dean of Westminster Abbey from 1986-1996, as well as in other prestigious prior postings, Mayne's name recognition is very different in his homeland than in North America. Indeed, in the United Kingdom his books have qualified as bestsellers in the category of spirituality.

Since discovering Mayne's writings for myself, thanks to the introduction by George Connor, reading and rereading each volume has been instructive, inspiring, and a pleasure. In preparation for this particular project, I have read Mayne's other published works including, his much less well-known books, and the relatively few other pieces (articles, reviews, introductions, and chapters in other authors' works) he penned. Mayne only began to publish relatively late in his career, thus his corpus, though significant, is not nearly as voluminous as, for instance, his friend Buechner's, or other prolific authors such as Thomas Merton, Henri Nouwen, etc. Mayne clearly understood his vocation first and foremost to be that of priest and pastor. The writing, though clearly deeply important to him, was secondary to his primary calling as a priest in the Church of England.

The Sources Consulted section includes dozens of citations of secondary sources on Mayne's work – reviews, articles, and obituaries written in response to his death from cancer of the jaw in October 2006. In addition to the pieces on Mayne himself, dozens of other spiritual works are cited which, in one way or another, help to shed light on his work by means of comparison or contrast. Mayne himself was extraordinarily well read. Before his own death, our mutual friend George Connor once remarked to me in a handwritten note regarding Mayne, "He seems to have read everything!" Comparing Mayne's writings to a broad cross section of (overtly or more subtly) other spiritual writings is in keeping with the breadth of Mayne's own vast reading. What follows is offered as an introduction to (for those unfamiliar with) and overview of the five major writings of Michael Mayne – *A Year Lost and Found* (1987, reissued in 2007); *This Sunrise of Wonder* (1995, reissued in 2008); *Pray, Love, Remember* (1998); *Learning to Dance* (2001); and *The Enduring Melody* (2006). Included is analysis of Mayne's work – its particular strengths and its contributions to the spiritual literature of the late twentieth and early twenty-first centuries. In the end the aim in offering this work is to guide new readers to, and those already familiar with Mayne back to, his writings themselves.

The author is particularly indebted to Michael Mayne's wife, Alison, for her very gracious encouragement regarding this project. Alison has offered me unfettered access to her husband's own very meticulously kept files on each of the five books. Additionally, I am deeply and lastingly grateful to her for the series of leisurely and wide-ranging conversations we enjoyed in their home in Salisbury, Wiltshire, in late September 2008. Alison is supportive of this work in every possible way and has helped very considerably in my bringing it into being.

Joel W. Huffstetler
St. George Island, Florida
The Feast of the Epiphany, 2009

ACKNOWLEDGMENTS

A number of friends and colleagues have contributed significantly to the work leading up to this book and are deserving of thanks. In the earliest stages, Peter Eaton, Alex Viola, and Colin Semper spoke with me by phone regarding the appropriateness of a volume focused on the writings of Michael Mayne. Rowan Williams, Anthony Harvey, John Austin Baker, Frederick Buechner, and Barry Morgan corresponded with me regarding Mayne's work and were exceptionally gracious in sharing their thoughts on his writings. Barrie Hibbert and John Waller read the first draft with great care and offered their encouragement regarding the project in the most helpful of ways via extended email conversations. Brendan Walsh supported my research most graciously and helpfully, and our conversation over breakfast in London enhanced my knowledge of Michael Mayne's writings immensely. Nicholas Sagovsky offered copies of his series of sermons in memory of Michael Mayne and was encouraging of this volume at every turn. John Hall, Jane Hedges, and June Osborne very graciously met with me during my research and were most helpful. Christina Shewell and Elizabeth Vardaman have the great advantage over me of having known Michael Mayne, and they remain dear friends of Alison's. Christina's Foreword and Elizabeth's Afterword enhance this volume greatly, and they have my most sincere gratitude. The people of St. Paul's Episcopal Church, Chattanooga, Tennessee, and St. Luke's Episcopal Church, Cleveland, Tennessee, have studied Michael Mayne's books with me and have encouraged my continued interest in his work, and I am grateful to them for their wonderful love and support. Rick Mathis encourages my interest in writing, and his own work instructs and inspires me. My thanks to Brenda Martin, who can read my mind and (astonishingly!) my handwriting. Brenda typed the earliest drafts of this work with her usual extraordinary expertise and care. Thanks to Geneie Grant, the other half of the St. Luke's 'Dream Team', for her very important help with this project. Thanks to Pam Boaz and Brenda Hooper, who very patiently and expertly edited the first draft of this project. Sheffey Gregory and Mark Shoop proofread this work at an intermediate stage and were exceedingly helpful. My thanks to Patti Williams, John Tallman, and Michael Doty for reading the final draft so carefully and helpfully. Thanks are due to Larry and Armen Epperson, as the majority of the work leading up to this volume took place at "About Time." Samantha Kirk is my editor at University Press of America and is wonderfully helpful in every way possible. Thank you, Samantha.

Acknowledgments

My wife, Debbie, encouraged this project at every stage of its life and typed the final, camera-ready version with love, care, and expertise. Thank you, my love.

Alison Mayne had never met me until I appeared at her door in September of 2008. Alison's support and facilitation of my study of her husband's writings have exceeded anything I could have hoped for or imagined. This book is dedicated to her.

INTRODUCTION

In its marking of the death of Michael Mayne, the obituary in *The Times* stated that he was "one of the most able, influential and hardworking priests of his generation."[1] Such was his influence that nearly all of the major newspapers in the United Kingdom acknowledged his passing. From very humble beginnings, Michael Mayne rose through the ranks of the Church of England and served at its highest levels with distinction. His final three postings were among the most visible and the most influential ministries in the church – Director of Religious Programmes for BBC Radio, Vicar of Great St. Mary's (The University Church), Cambridge, and Dean of Westminster Abbey. During his tenure at Westminster, Mayne's profile in the Church of England would have been as high as nearly any other figure, save the archbishops of Canterbury and York. The wording of the obituary in *The Times* is apt. Michael Mayne was, without question, one of the Church of England's most able clerics. His influence continues and includes the thousands of readers of his five major books. Michael Mayne was indeed a hard worker, a dedicated and conscientious priest, and a pastor at heart who, by the end of his life, had also come to be recognized as one of the finest spiritual writers of his generation in the United Kingdom.

Peter Eaton, who first knew Mayne when he (Mayne) was Vicar of St. George's, Norton, Letchworth, states that Mayne was a "consummate pastor" while also being a writer of "remarkable sensitivity and grace."[2] Mayne's colleague at Westminster, Anthony Harvey, in an obituary for Mayne in *The Tablet*, very graciously acknowledges Mayne's giftedness regarding pastoral ministry but adds, "Many will be grateful to him especially as a writer."[3] Commenting on the breadth of Mayne's reading and how his books are a blend of poetry, prose, music, as well as theology, but theology in a very practical, accessible sense, Rowan Williams observes that in his writings Mayne "values the entire life of the imagination," finding the 'real' theology, as often as not, in works not explicitly theological in nature.[4]

One of the consistent themes running throughout Mayne's writing is that of being observant in the moment, of being grateful for all of life's blessings – from the seemingly small blessings, easy to overlook or to take for granted, to life's more obvious, more dramatic blessings. John Waller was Vicar of Harpenden when Mayne returned there to live while commuting into London daily for his work with the BBC. Mayne had been a curate at Harpenden earlier in his career, and he was asked to preach the sermon in Westminster when his

friend Waller was ordained a bishop. In a summary comment on the sweep of
Mayne's writings, Waller notes that his friend "longed for us all to have our ears
tuned and our eyes open."[5]

Mayne urges his readers to find joy in life, to be filled with gratitude to
God for all of the wonders of creation, and to experience the love made known
to us through the grace of God, revealed most completely in Jesus. But Mayne's
counsel toward gratitude and thankfulness is balanced by an acute awareness of
the reality of pain and suffering. He readily acknowledges that life is inevitably
a mixture of joy and sadness, and he understands that writing about the beauty
of life in this world must at the same time honestly reckon with its harshness.
The Times obituary states that Mayne's books are "attractive weaves of poetry,
science, and spirituality, with uninhibited analyses of suffering, others' and his
own."[6] In her bestselling book, *Traveling Mercies: Some Thoughts on Faith*,
Anne Lamott quotes her son Sam, then aged 7, who opined, "I think I already
understand about life: pretty good, some problems."[7] Mayne's works deal
honestly, forthrightly, and unrelentingly realistically with both the goodness, and
the difficulties of human existence. His very candid recounting of his
devastating experience of Myalgic Encephalomyelitis (ME), more commonly
referred to as chronic fatigue syndrome, in his book *A Year Lost and Found* is as
detailed and as revealing a description of life in that condition as exists in the
general literature on the subject. And in his final book, *The Enduring Melody*,
Mayne courageously deals with the realities of his once hopeful battle with
cancer as the prognosis turns from optimistic to terminal.

In a sermon preached at a requiem eucharist for the life of Mayne in
Mayne's former parish, Great St. Mary's (The University Church), Cambridge,
Eamon Duffy notes that Mayne, "Produced a series of beautiful books, distilled
from his love of literature and art, and filled with wisdom and humanity born out
of his own first-hand knowledge of the woundedness of the human spirit."[8] He
continues, "The books conveyed the man – sensitive, immensely widely read,
self-deprecatingly humorous, filled with celebration, as well as, underneath it
all, the acknowledgement of pain...."[9] It is indeed rare to find a writer who
deals with both the joys of life as well as its pain as adroitly as does Michael
Mayne. It is with an appreciation for Mayne's unusual skill in this that Barry
Morgan states, "I find all his works incredibly illuminating."[10]

Throughout his life Mayne held on to an interest in and love of acting,
an interest born in his youth. While a student at the King's School, Canterbury,
Mayne played the lead role of Hamlet to rave reviews. His love of the stage in
part helped Mayne to be especially comfortable and adept at public speaking,
and he was, consequently, in much demand as a speaker, guest preacher, and
guest lecturer. Remembering his several speaking engagements at Baylor
University in Waco, Texas, Mayne's friend Elizabeth Vardaman recalls that he
was a "riveting" speaker.[11] Listening to Mayne's contributions to the 1996
Bowen Lectures is confirmation of his giftedness for the spoken, as well as the
written word. His meditations flow seamlessly from one subject to the next and
are delivered with an actor's sensibility, i.e., with the hearer in mind.

Interspersed at appropriate points in both his talks and his books is humor. Mayne had a wonderful, very apparent quick wit, and he clearly understood the need not to take himself too seriously. Mayne's talks during the Bowen Lectures can elicit uproarious laughter, and then, again with an actor's skill, he can turn the subject to a matter of the utmost poignancy.

Unquestionably, Mayne was gifted with a particularly keen intellect. His vast reading was not only broad in scope, but was deeply insightful. His friends remember him as one who had the grace to wear his learning lightly. Along these lines one is reminded of the dialogue between Katharine Tynan and Gerard Manley Hopkins, recounted in Frederick Buechner's *Speak What We Feel (Not What We Ought to Say): Reflections on Literature and Faith*. Katharine quizzes Hopkins as to how was it that a man like him, with all his obvious interest in literature and the arts, had decided to become of all things a priest![12] Hopkins responds, "You wouldn't give only the dull ones to Almighty God."[13] Mayne's intellect was such that he was doubtless one of the most respected priests in the Church of England. In a column on the noted scholar, Nathan A. Scott, Jr., George Connor notes that Scott was once in charge of a continuing education program for what he (Scott) called, "the reading clergy." Delightfully and poignantly, Connor observes that the reading clergy is "a fine distinction but not all inclusive."[14] Michael Mayne, as his books clearly evince, was the quintessential reading clergy.

Michael Clement Otway Mayne was born 10 September 1929 in Harlestone, Northamptonshire. His father was the parish priest in Harlestone. Mayne's life was changed forever when in 1933 his father committed suicide. On a Saturday afternoon, while Mayne was with his mother in the village, his father climbed up into the church's belfry and threw himself down to his death, which was almost immediate. Mayne's father had left a brief note, and 40 GBP in the bank. Mayne's mother, having to vacate the rectory, moved with her son Michael to her mother's room in a hotel beside St. Marylebone station in London. Afterwards, she set up a small boarding house. Before going away to boarding school, Mayne and his mother lived a life with precious few advantages. Theirs has been described as a life of poverty. It was during his disadvantaged youth that Mayne's love of reading was born as an escape from the harsh realities of his daily life. Mayne's keen intellect in time became evident, and through the benevolence of clergy charities, he was able to attend the excellent King's School, Canterbury, from 1942 – 1949. There he pursued his love of acting, as well as excelling in his academic work.

In *Speak What We Feel (Not What We Ought to Say): Reflections on Literature and Faith,* Frederick Buechner writes of, "The dark shadow that my father's suicide continues to cast over my days even now that more than sixty-five years have passed since it occurred in my childhood."[15] Buechner and Mayne became dear friends in large part, at first, through the common experience of their fathers having committed suicide. Buechner's latest book, *The Yellow Leaves: A Miscellany*, is dedicated to Alison Mayne and is in memory of Michael. In his later works, Mayne deals very candidly with the effects that his father's suicide had on his life. In an obituary for his friend and colleague, Anthony Harvey notes that Mayne's life was one "deeply marked" by losing his father so tragically at such a young age.[16]

After his time of national service in the Royal Airforce, Mayne was enrolled in Corpus Christi College, Cambridge, where he read English and Theology and was active in drama – so much so, in fact, that he seriously considered a career in theatre. It was his former headmaster at the King's School, Canon John Shirley, who wrote to Mayne, "You're not going to be an actor: you're going to be a priest." Mayne did indeed choose the church and attended theological college at Cuddesdon, graduating in 1957. He served as a curate at St. John's, Harpenden, (diocese of St. Alban's) from 1957 – 1959. Mayne enjoyed ministry in Harpenden and relocated his family there when he was appointed Director of Religious Programmes for BBC Radio.

From Harpenden, Mayne was appointed as Domestic Chaplain to Mervyn Stockwood, Bishop of Southwark, serving from 1959 – 1965. Stockwood's biographer, Michael De-la-Noy, notes that Mayne was "just one of a truly astonishing string of men whose talent Mervyn spotted early on in their careers...."[17] The years 1959 – 1965 were a heady time to be at the center of life in the diocese of Southwark. These were the days of the so-called "South Bank Religion," a time of intense theological dialogue and liturgical experimentation in Southwark. John A. T. Robinson's *Honest to God* was published in 1963. Robinson was Bishop of Woolwich at the time, a close friend of Michael's, and in time would become Sarah Mayne's godfather. Life in the diocese of Southwark was fast paced, and Bishop Stockwood relied heavily on the services of his domestic chaplain. De-la-Noy writes, "Mervyn always looked back upon Mayne's period at Bishop's House as utopian."[18]

In an obituary for Mayne in *Church Times*, his friend and colleague Donald Gray recalls that for Mayne, in the service of Bishop Stockwood in the days of South Bank Religion, life was "never less than exciting...."[19] Mayne himself recounts in De-la-Noy's biography of his mentor, "I loved being chaplain and would not have missed it for anything. I learned a huge amount about how the church works, some of it for good, some of it for ill."[20] De-la-Noy writes of Stockwood that beneath the "showman" there was in Stockwood "consistently a pastoral heart, and a pastoral care for people that went very deep."[21] This is consistent with Mayne's own estimate of Stockwood's pastoral inclinations, and it is important to note that some thirty years on, while serving as Dean of furiously paced Westminster, Mayne was recognized by clergy colleagues, as well as by Abbey staff and volunteers, to be first and foremost a pastor.

Near the end of his tenure in Southwark, Mayne married Alison McKie in Southwark Cathedral in 1965. The Maynes have two children, Sarah and Mark, and four grandchildren.

From Southwark, Mayne went to be the vicar of St. George's, Norton, Letchworth (diocese of St. Alban's), serving from 1965 – 1972. To Norton, Mayne carried with him an embrace of many of the ideas of South Bank

Religion, and he enjoyed his tenure there in very much a working class environment. While in Norton, Mayne published his first book, *The Norton Prayer Book* (1970), a compilation of one hundred prayers, nine of which are of Mayne's own composition. Thirty-seven years after Mayne left Norton as Vicar, a prayer group he founded during his time there continues to meet.

While the vicar of Norton, Mayne participated in a continuing education program for clergy administered through St. George's House, Windsor Castle. On the strength of a paper Mayne wrote for the course, and with no practical experience in broadcasting, Mayne was chosen as Director of Religious Programmes for BBC Radio, serving from 1972 – 1979. The family lived in Harpenden, and Mayne commuted to his office in London.

In 1979 came Mayne's appointment as the vicar of Great St. Mary's (The University Church), Cambridge, one of the most visible pulpits in the Church of England. Mayne's immediate predecessors at Great St. Mary's included the likes of Mervyn Stockwood and Hugh Montefiore. Mayne welcomed the return to parish ministry, and he thrived in the intellectual environs of Cambridge. The pace of ministry there, however, did take its toll. Surprisingly, in retrospect Mayne found the demands of ministry in Great St. Mary's to be more draining and more stressful than those of being Dean of Westminster, due in large part to the army of clergy and lay staff as well as volunteers who support the ministry of the abbey. While at Great St. Mary's, Mayne organized a quite ambitious conference titled "Encounters," an ecumenical gathering which included speakers from a wide variety of faith perspectives. The conference ran for eight days in February 1985. One of the speakers was a young theologian named Rowan Williams. The conference's addresses were compiled in a book titled, *Encounters: Exploring Christian Faith*, which Mayne edited, and to which he contributed an introduction. In the introduction Mayne writes of the conference, "Not least, we wanted people to understand better the legitimate breadth and space of faith and discipleship and the need for diverse and complementary insights in our encounter with God."[22] Anticipating his later and much more well-known works, Mayne observes, "Only a form of belief which fully engages the mind as well as the heart can survive in the real world, where the innocent suffers and where those we love fall ill and die."[23] Late in his tenure in Cambridge, Mayne was struck with ME. His experiences with that debilitating illness gave rise to his first major book, *A Year Lost and Found*.

In November of 1985 during the latter stages of his bout with ME, Mayne received a package marked "Strictly private and confidential."[24] The package contained a letter from the Prime Minister, inviting Mayne to allow his name to go forward for the Deanery of Westminster. In time it was decided that his health would allow him to undertake the ministry of overseeing the work of one of the most visible and dynamic centers of worship in the world. Mayne served as Dean from 1986 – 1996, during which time he wrote *A Year Lost and Found* and *This Sunrise of Wonder*. In 1996 he also published a much less well-known booklet, *Something Understood: Talks on Prayer*.

Anthony Harvey recalls that though Mayne brought a "rich array of other gifts to the task," at the heart of his ministry at the abbey was that basic commitment, assumed at his ordination as priest of the Church of England, "To maintain and promote dignified and relevant public worship supported by a sustained and comprehensive pastoral ministry."[25] It was Mayne's desire to make the abbey more obviously a place of prayer – no small task, as the abbey draws some two million visitors a year, many of whom come strictly as tourists, with no overtly spiritual interest in the abbey as a functioning church. To the abbey Mayne brought his fundamental orientation as a parish priest, and worship would be at the very top of his priorities list. During his tenure as Dean, Mayne was comfortable delegating an appropriate amount of the detailed administration of the abbey to colleagues and staff, allowing him to function as a pastoral presence. Colleagues, staff, volunteers, and countless Londoners came to Mayne for counsel. During his ten years as Dean, Mayne demonstrated particular concern for people with HIV and AIDS before such care had become the norm in ecclesiastical circles. Three times a year persons with HIV/AIDS and their carers were invited to a buffet supper in the abbey's Jerusalem Chamber, followed by an after-hours tour of the abbey, ending with prayer. Through the years a number of well-known actors came to the abbey to present "Personal Choice" evenings (poetry readings), attracting large audiences and raising many thousands of pounds for AIDS charities. In addition to issues surrounding HIV/AIDS, Mayne was particularly keen that the abbey be involved with issues involving refugees and asylum seekers, as well as those who were victims of torture. He also helped to facilitate a support group for London clergy called the Central Line Group. Upon his retirement from Westminster in 1996, Mayne was appointed a Knight of the Royal Victorian Order (KVCO).

The Maynes retired to Salisbury in 1996, and Dean Mayne was much in demand as a speaker in a variety of forums. In 'retirement' he wrote three books – *Pray, Love, Remember* (1998); *Learning to Dance* (2001); and *The Enduring Melody* (2006). In the latter stages of retirement, Mayne experienced a recurrence of ME. Just as he was recovering from this bout with chronic fatigue syndrome, he was diagnosed with cancer. Mayne endured this final struggle with courage and with dignity. He died at the age of 77 on 22 October 2006.

Notes

1. Obituary for Michael Mayne, *The Times*, 25 October 2006, 68.
2. Peter Eaton, "A Rich Life: The Writings of Michael Mayne," *The Living Church* 234 (6 May 2007): 18.
3. Anthony Harvey, Obituary for Michael Mayne, *The Tablet*, 4 November 2006, 40.
4. Rowan Williams, Personal correspondence, 13 November 2007.
5. John Waller, Personal correspondence, 8 December 2008.
6. *The Times*, 25 October 2006, 68.

7. Anne Lamott, *Traveling Mercies: Some Thoughts on Faith* (New York: Pantheon Books, 1999), 145.

8. Eamon Duffy, sermon preached at Great St. Mary's (The University Church), Cambridge, for a Eucharist of Remembering and Thanksgiving for Michael Mayne, 22 January 2007, 6.

9. Ibid.

10. Barry Morgan, Personal correspondence, 20 March 2008.

11. Elizabeth Vardaman, Personal correspondence, 30 December 2008.

12. Frederick Buechner, *Speak What We Feel (Not What We Ought to Say): Reflections on Literature and Faith* (New York: HarperSanFrancisco, 2001), 3.

13. Ibid., 4.

14. George Connor, *Hints and Guesses II: Selected Commentaries, 1982 – 1997* (Chattanooga, TN: St. Peter's Episcopal Church, 1997), 107.

15. Buechner, *Speak What We Feel (Not What We Ought to Say): Reflections on Literature and Faith,* 159.

16. Anthony Harvey, Obituary for Michael Mayne, *The Independent on Sunday*, 28 October 2006.

17. Michael De-la-Noy, *Mervyn Stockwood: A Lonely Life* (London: Mowbray, 1996), 107.

18. Ibid., 175.

19. Donald Gray, Obituary for Michael Mayne, *Church Times*, 27 October 2006, 27.

20. De-la-Noy, 175.

21. Ibid., 176.

22. Michael Mayne, ed., *Encounters: Exploring Christian Faith* (London: Darton, Longman and Todd, 1987), 26.

23. Ibid., 1.

24. Michael Mayne, *A Year Lost and Found* (London: Darton, Longman and Todd, 1987), 26.

25. Harvey, Obituary for Michael Mayne, *The Independent on Sunday*, 1.

CHAPTER ONE

A YEAR LOST AND FOUND

In 1987 Michael Mayne published *A Year Lost and Found*, his reflections on his debilitating experience with ME in the midst of a very busy and fulfilling life as Vicar of Great St. Mary's, Cambridge. Darton, Longman and Todd issued a subsequent edition in 2007 featuring a new foreword by Sister Frances Dominica. The foreword in the original edition is by Gerald Priestland. *A Year Lost and Found* has garnered a niche audience among those affected in one way or another by ME. The book has 'legs' twenty-two years after it first appeared.

The Times obituary for Mayne refers to *A Year Lost and Found* as a "small masterpiece."[1] Mayne's friend Nicholas Sagovsky notes that the book "is like an overture to the symphonic variations in Michael's later books," and that all the big themes, which he later developed much more fully are there in *A Year Lost and Found*.[2] Readers appreciate the fact that Mayne is able to be honest and forthright regarding his struggle with ME without being unduly self-centered, unhelpfully sentimental, and without abandoning proper reticence. In her review of the book, Stephanie Sorréll remarks that it is written with "dignity, heart and vision."[3] The obituary for Mayne posted on the Westminster Abbey website includes the observation by Robert Wright that in *A Year Lost and Found*, Mayne breaks the pattern of members of the British establishment who typically do not allow their public persona to show weakness or vulnerability. Consequently, the book has helped "countless" people suffering from ME.[4] In the obituary written for *The Church of England Newspaper*, John Barton observes that the book "quickly became a classic for fellow-sufferers, many of whom had hitherto felt themselves ostracised simply because their illness was – and still is – something of a mystery."[5] While reviewing *The Enduring Melody* in *The Observer*, Robert McCrum mentions that Mayne's first major book continues to be helpful to ME sufferers "worldwide."[6] Peter Eaton goes so far as to assert that *A Year Lost and Found* is "one of the best reflections on illness and suffering."[7]

In an undated article written for the Guild of St. Raphael website, Mayne states, "There have been [at that time] three other books, somewhat more ambitious and diverse, yet (frustratingly!) it's the ME book that people most often write about...."[8] Here Mayne is modest about the amount of mail generated by his other books. In his files are dozens of letters from appreciative readers the world over. Having said that, however, it is true that *A Year Lost and Found* has struck a chord with the largest number of readers. One letter's key line sums up literally hundreds of other letters from readers who have found solace in *A Year Lost and Found*: "No answer needed: just soak up the gratitude."

Gerald Priestland, who had worked for Mayne at the BBC, writes in the foreword that an old teacher of his used to insist, "No experience is ever wasted," and such is the message of *A Year Lost and Found*.[9] He observes that one of the key strengths of the book is that Mayne speaks of suffering to readers from a genuine experience of suffering and not simply from what his theological studies have taught him.[10] Priestland notes that even the risen Christ still bore the wounds of the nails and the spear in his resurrection body, and that Mayne's counsel through his reflections in *A Year Lost and Found* is that though suffering is real, it is not a "dead end."[11]

In introducing the book, Mayne asserts from the beginning that it is a very personal reflection on one year of his life.[12] Over the years, and in various contexts, Mayne remarks that honest, authentic, 'personal' books are the only kind worth writing or reading. He recalls offering speakers at Great St. Mary's the counsel, "If it is in your nature to do so, be a little vulnerable. Don't be afraid to talk about yourself, *your* journey, *your* pain, *your* vision."[13] Here readers encounter one of Mayne's key themes running throughout his writing – self-acceptance, certainly not an indulgent sense of self-importance, but an honest, realistic, healthy acceptance of one's uniqueness, and one's value in the eyes of God. This theme is fleshed out fully in *This Sunrise of Wonder* but is also a key part of the foundational mindset underlying *A Year Lost and Found*. In his first major book, Mayne is practicing what he had 'preached' for years regarding an appropriate and healthy vulnerability. He states that the book is a forthright attempt to describe his experience of vulnerability.[14] In his article "M. E.," Mayne writes:

> Professionalism may properly involve a holding back of large parts of oneself, yet (as Wordsworth wrote) 'we all share one human heart' and there are times when we need to share our stories as a way of affirming our common humanity and helping to authenticate what others may be going through.[15]

Mayne's files on *A Year Lost and Found* contain an untitled, undated, unpaginated typed manuscript in which he discusses the book. The manuscript includes his observation that C. S. Lewis' book *A Grief Observed*, which records Lewis' reaction to his wife's death from cancer, is written with such acknowledgment of pain and perplexity that when it was first published Lewis chose that it should go out under a pseudonym. Mayne notes:

> *A Grief Observed* by N. W. Clark is the title on my copy. And yet I suspect that for a good many people it is his raw and honest account of the gradual shuffling towards some kind of faith that makes it the Lewis book they treasure most.[16]

He continues:

> My belief is that, if we are to use words to communicate with each other at
> any but the most trivial level, we must shed our natural shyness and share
> some of our human experience a little more freely, and help each other find
> meaning in it. To be honest without egotism and without abandoning proper
> reticence is hard, yet the attempt is worth making. 'Don't you feel it's a bit
> like undressing in public' a friend asked after my book [*A Year Lost and
> Found*] had been published. No, I don't; I prefer to see it as an attempt to share
> our common humanity.[17]

Nicholas Sagovsky gave the sermon at Mayne's memorial service in
Westminster Abbey. In the sermon he recalls the advice Mayne offers in *A Year
Lost and Found* regarding vulnerability. Sagovsky notes that this is exactly
what Mayne himself did in each of his books and, "This is what touched people
so deeply."[18]

In his biography of John A. T. Robinson, Eric James recalls Phillips
Brooks' description of preaching as "the communication of truth through
personality."[19] Such an understanding undergirds Mayne's counsel as recorded
in *A Year Lost and Found*. A speaker communicates truth, rather than mere
ideas or concepts, through the truth of the speaker's own life experiences. And
listeners are more able to hear the truth when it is spoken from the speaker's
own authentic, vulnerable, and deeply honest storehouse of life experiences.

Henri Nouwen addresses this subject of self-acceptance and its
importance in being able to communicate the gospel message most
compellingly. Writing in *Befriending Life: Encounters with Henri Nouwen*,
Wendy Lywood recalls Nouwen's advice to her during an ordination retreat:

> Wendy, remember the ministry is about being present with people as you are,
> not as you are not. You won't say anything new or original, just speak from
> your heart and from your own relationship with Jesus. You're not there to solve
> problems but to announce that Jesus wants to love, heal, forgive, and
> reconcile.[20]

In reflecting on this aspect of Nouwen's teaching, Michael O'Laughlin writes:

> [Nouwen's] considerable contribution to Christian spirituality was based on a
> decision renewed again and again, to be true to himself. If life is a response to
> God's love, then part of our response is to see ourselves, be ourselves, own
> who we are, and speak from our hearts.[21]

O'Laughlin continues, "Henri's personal spirituality revolved around his
realizing and embracing his own identity."[22]

In the preface to Nouwen's *Turn My Mourning into Dancing: Moving
Through Hard Times with Hope*, Timothy Jones writes of Nouwen's "broken
heart" which was opened for his fellow friends and readers through Nouwen's

own deeply personal writing. Jones notes, "Henri was complex and unfinished; he knew it well and did not pretend otherwise." [23]

Nouwen himself writes, "When you befriend your true self and discover that it is good and beautiful, you will see Jesus there."[24] Readers familiar with the broad sweep of Nouwen's work will realize that he struggled mightily to befriend his true self in all circumstances. But his honesty regarding the struggle to bring this concept of self-acceptance into a consistent application is a very large part of what makes Nouwen's writings, particularly his journals, so compelling – they are unflinchingly, at times uncomfortably, honest reflections on his struggle to put what he preaches into action in his own life. Nouwen remembers the advice that a friend gave him regarding a proposed book on spirituality: "Speak from that place in your heart where you are most yourself. Speak directly, simply, lovingly, gently and without any apologies."[25] The friend's counsel concludes, "Trust your own heart. The words will come. There is nothing to fear."[26]

Readers familiar with both Mayne and Nouwen will know that Mayne's very personal words are absolutely as honest as those of Nouwen, but are more reserved. It is often joked regarding Nouwer   er had a thought he didn't publish. Such is certainly not the case   Michael Mayne, who was reticent to say too much about himself for fear of becoming tiresomely repetitive or appearing to be self-indulgent.   Despite their differences in personality and temperament, at a foundational level, Mayne and Nouwen make the same point – what we have in us to express regarding Christian truths is best and most compellingly conveyed honestly, personally, and with integrity.

Frederick Buechner addresses the subject of self-acceptance in ways similar to his dear friend Mayne. In *A Room Called Remember: Uncollected Pieces*, Buechner writes:

> You learn as much as you can from the wise until finally, if you do it right and things break your way, you are wise enough to be yourself, and brave enough to speak with your own voice, and foolish enough, for Christ's sake, to live and serve out of the uniqueness of your own vision of him and out of your own passion.[27]

In *Telling Secrets*, Buechner suggests that one best speaks the truth of the gospel "not the way you would compose an essay but the way you would write a poem or a love letter...."[28]   As an example of the power of speaking from a very personal, authentic standpoint, Buechner cites the early writings of William Maxwell. According to Buecher:

> His first novel, *Bright Center of Heaven*, written in 1934 when he was twenty-six, is derivative and unconvincing, but in *They Came Like Swallows*, based on memories of his mother's death from Spanish influenza during the epidemic of 1918 when he was ten, he is clearly and powerfully speaking in his own true voice out of the deepest truth of his own life....[29]

The final phrase of the quotation is key to the understanding running throughout Mayne's five major books – in them Mayne is speaking *clearly* and *powerfully* in *his own true voice*, and *out of the deepest truths* of his own life. The counsel he gave to anxious speakers at Great St. Mary's is counsel he himself follows in his writings. In his book *Empowering Ministry: Ways to Grow in Effectiveness*, Donald P. Smith states, "Overwhelming evidence confirms that open integrity is always the core of effectiveness."[30] What one finds in Mayne's books is a quintessential example of open integrity.

Following the preface, *A Year Lost and Found* is divided into two parts, Part I being a kind of diary recording the events of May 1985 to April 1986, and Part II containing Mayne's considered reflections on his experiences with ME and the lessons learned he intends to carry forward. Early on in Part I he recalls writing a letter to the parish explaining his disability due to the mysterious illness plaguing him. In response a friend wrote back, "At least it will give you time to pray."[31] Mayne records his own (private) response, "But no; when you are ill you need others within the Body to do that for you."[32] Here is an important reminder regarding life in a community of faith, where it is crucial for those who are able to come to the aid of those who are either permanently or temporarily in difficult circumstances. Mayne was, at this point, unable to concentrate on his prayers. He was overwhelmed at the sudden reversal of fortune he was experiencing. And so this period was not a time of intense prayer for him; it was a time to be intensely prayed for, a time to be upheld by, as he puts it, the Body.

In *The Yellow Leaves: A Miscellany*, Frederick Buechner recalls that while a youth in Washington, DC, he once was in the lobby of a hotel when President Franklin Delano Roosevelt and his delegation were present. Buechner recalls seeing how the 'powerful' President of the United States was, in fact, dependent on his braces, and on the support of those persons around him in whom he trusted. Buechner notes: "What I learned for the first time from that glimpse I had of him in the elevator is that even the mightiest among us can't stand on our own. Unless we have someone to hold us, our flimsy legs buckle."[33]

A part of Mayne's record of his battle with ME is the issue of visitors, and the question of how best to offer gestures of love and support to those who are seriously ill. For him, visitors were sometimes a problem, however thoughtful and sensitive they might have been, as they were "tiring" for him, given his weakened condition.[34] He goes on to discuss the art of visiting the sick, stressing the importance of being truly present to the person who is ill, giving of oneself and being deeply interested in the person's condition. Mayne offers counsel based on his experiences on how best to visit and be helpfully supportive to the person who is ill without being tiring, staying too long, or, consciously or subconsciously, shifting attention away from the person being visited and onto oneself.[35] He stresses that though visits should not be overly long or tiring for the person being visited, persons who are ill do need reassuring that they are not isolated from the community, and he articulates the vital need of those who are ill for both touch and prayer. Put succinctly, "I believe that most of us, when we are sick, need physical contact and the spoken assurance of God's love."[36]

Mayne admits that at about midpoint during his illness he became deeply frustrated and that it was hard for him not to feel disappointed and frustrated with God. He questioned, "What are you doing to me, God? I long to be well: I put my trust in your healing power: why are you so slow?"[37]

In Part II Mayne reflects on the lessons learned from his struggle with ME, and early on in his reflections is an important reminder that when one is ill it is crucial that such a person be treated as a *person*, rather than a set of symptoms. For all of the marvelous benefits of modern, specialized medicine, one of the dangers is that in the specialized, clinical treatment approaches which have become the norm, the *person* being treated may become lost amidst the sometimes fragmented, though clinically expert, specialized care. Perceptively, Mayne notes that the increased interest in alternative medicine is not merely a fringe movement but is an expression of the awareness that in much of modern medicine what was once assumed regarding the traditional doctor/patient relationship (i.e., treatment of the whole person) is in danger of being lost.[38]

One of the major learnings Mayne intends to carry forward following his illness is a renewed sense of thanksgiving for the gift of life itself. Mayne intends to go forward with an increasingly grateful heart. This will prove to be the theme of his second major book, *This Sunrise of Wonder*, but the essence of his thinking on the subject is present in *A Year Lost and Found*. Foundational to Mayne's understanding of gratitude is a quotation from Paul van Buren's *Theological Foundations*, which reads:

> What marks off...the deep ones from the superficial...[is] their sense of wonder, awe, and joy before what is there for all to behold; the fact that we are alive, that there is anything at all....This sense of awe and wonder occurs when one is *struck* by the fact that I am, and that I am I, that a tree is itself, that there is anything at all.[39]

The thrust of Mayne's reflections on his illness is that, having experienced its pain, confusion, and frustration, one emerges from illness with a renewed appreciation for the blessings in life which a healthy person can unwittingly take for granted. Returning to health, Mayne wishes to experience life once again with a child's sense of wonder, joy, and contentedness to live life 'in the moment' rather than being resentful about the past or anxious about the future. He observes, "To do that, of course, presupposes an immense trust in the order of things."[40] Mayne articulates freely that, intellectually, he has understood the idea of living 'in the moment' for years, but, having survived his illness, his intention is to move forward being *truly* thankful for each moment, content to enjoy what each 'now' brings.[41]

In *A Year Lost and Found* Mayne is very candid regarding his understanding of the cross of Christ, and the central role that the cross plays in his theology, particularly as it informs his theological response to his recent incapacitation. Mayne's theology is grounded in an acceptance that pain and suffering are realities in life and that Christian theology must, and indeed does, deal with this reality straightforwardly. For him, the message of the cross is that God is with us *in* our suffering, and that we are not abandoned by God when we suffer just as Jesus himself was not abandoned by God on the cross. For Mayne, *compassion* is at the very heart of Christian theology, the word's most foundational meaning being to suffer alongside. He writes, "If I were to sum up in a sentence why I am a Christian (let alone a priest) I would say that it is because I believe in the Passion of Jesus Christ and the compassion of God."[42]

In his book, *The Foolishness of God*, Mayne's dear friend John Austin Baker writes, "The cross is not a picture of God. This was God himself."[43] In *What Was God Doing on the Cross?*, Alister McGrath agrees that the cross is a "potent symbol of Christian realism. It declares that any outlook on life which cannot cope with the grim realities of suffering and death does not deserve to get a hearing."[44] McGrath continues:

> This symbol of suffering and death affirms that Christianity faces up to the grim, ultimate realities of life. It reminds us of something we must never be allowed to forget. God entered into our suffering and dying in order to bring it newness of life.[45]

He adds that the cross "confronts the worst which the world can offer, and points to – and makes possible – a better way. It stands as a symbol of hope which transfigures, in a world which is too often tinged with sadness and tears."[46] Mayne's hope is grounded in Jesus, on the cross, facing up to, in McGrath's words, the grim, ultimate realities of life. Our hope lies in the fact that God in Christ is *with us* as we confront the worst that life can offer. As Peter Gomes puts it in *The Good Book: Reading the Bible with Mind and Heart,* "It is the most orthodox of Christian doctrine that the Savior does not save us *from* suffering, but is with us *in* and *through* suffering."[47]

One can argue that the contemporary writer most similar to Michael Mayne in approach and tone is Mark Oakley in his *The Collage of God*. Oakley is familiar with Mayne's work and in reading his (Oakley's) very fine book, one is unmistakably reminded of Mayne's writings. Regarding the cross Oakley says, "Christ on the cross displays a God taken out of all the wrappings we dress him in and puzzlingly unveils him and his suffering love against all our better judgement and understanding."[48]

Emerging from a year's illness, Mayne is intent on being a more compassionate person. He is keen to claim that no human being is in a position to stand in ultimate judgment of another, as, "That is God's prerogative, and his judgement is matched by his mercy."[49] Mayne's illness has served to reinforce his understanding that no one individual can fully understand the experience of another, and individuals simply cannot know for sure what their response would have been had they been in another person's shoes.[50] Though he certainly would not have chosen to go through a year of severe incapacitation through the devastating effects of ME, one can emerge from such an experience wiser, more tolerant, and, says Mayne, "Above all, more compassionate."[51]

* * *

In "M.E.," Mayne writes, "If you have tasted something of the dark shadowlands of sickness or pain or loss that most people enter at some point in their lives, then it will deepen your compassion."[52]   John O'Donohue notes similarly in *Eternal Echoes: Exploring Our Yearning to Belong*, "When you have felt and experienced pain, it refines the harshness that may be in you."[53] Interestingly, those who knew Michael Mayne well frequently use the word "gentle" in describing him.   Mayne's gentle, understanding, compassionate pastoral ministry was no doubt influenced greatly by his experience of the shadowlands of ME. One is reminded here of Charles Simeon, who regularly instructed his ministerial students in Cambridge, "Be gentle among your people...as a mother with her family."[54]

The titles of his books were especially important to Michael Mayne, thus much is to be gleaned from the title of his first major book, *A Year Lost and Found*. The year he suffered from ME was lost with regard to his active ministry, and to participation in something resembling a normal routine. But the year was not lost ultimately. He learned hard won life lessons which he carried with him for the rest of his life. And in sharing his experiences and insights through *A Year Lost and Found* he has comforted, encouraged, and inspired thousands of readers affected in one way or another by ME, for whom there is no other book quite like it. Though in one sense lost to Mayne, ultimately the year was found in the experience that God in Christ is with us in the midst of our very real pain, loss, and despair, and that through the crucified and risen Lord we are never outside of God's tender, understanding, compassionate love.

NOTES

1. Obituary for Michael Mayne, *The Times,* 68.
2. Nicholas Sagovsky, "A Year Lost and Found," sermon preached at Westminster Abbey, 5 November 2006, 5.
3. Stephanie Sorréll, review of *A Year Lost and Found,* by Michael Mayne, *The Review* (November/December 1994):187
4. Obituary for Michael Mayne, Westminster Abbey [on-line]. Available from http://www.westminster-abbey.org/article/;htm?article=20061022_mayne.inc.
5. John Barton, Obituary for Michael Mayne, *The Church of England Newspaper*, 3 November 2006, 28.
6. Robert McCrum, "Hope Lives on in Cancer Country," *The Observer*, 17 September 2006.

7. Peter Eaton, "A Rich Life: The Writings of Michael Mayne," 18.
8. Michael Mayne, "M.E. (Chronic Fatigue Syndrome)," [on-line]. Available from http://www.guild-of-st-raphael.org.uk/m_e_.htm.
9. Michael Mayne, *A Year Lost and Found*, vii.
10. Ibid., viii.
11. Ibid.
12. Ibid., 1.
13. Ibid., 2.
14. Ibid., 3.
15. Michael Mayne, "M.E. (Chronic Fatigue Syndrome)," 2.
16. Michael Mayne, unpublished essay on *A Year Lost and Found*.
17. Ibid.
18. Nicholas Sagovsky, sermon preached at Westminster Abbey for the Memorial Service for Michael Mayne, 1 February 2007, 1.
19. Eric James, *A Life of Bishop John A. T. Robinson: Scholar, Pastor, Prophet* (Grand Rapids: William B. Eerdmans Publishing Company, 1987), 304.
20. Wendy Lywood, "Rediscovering My Priesthood," in *Befriending Life: Encounters with Henri Nouwen,* ed. Beth Porter, with Susan M. S. Brown and Philip Coulter (New York: Image Books, 2001), 234.
21. Michael O'Laughlin, *God's Beloved: A Spiritual Biography of Henri Nouwen* (Maryknoll, NY: Orbis Books, 2004), 162.
22. Ibid.
23. Henri Nouwen, *Turn My Mourning into Dancing: Moving Through Hard Times with Hope* (Nashville: W Publishing Group, 2001), xi.
24. Henri Nouwen, *The Inner Voice of Love: A Journey Through Anguish to Freedom* (New York: Image Books, 1996), 49.
25. Henri Nouwen, *Life of the Beloved: Spiritual Living in a Secular World* (New York: Crossroad, 1992), 20.
26. Ibid.
27. Frederick Buechner, *A Room Called Remember: Uncollected Pieces* (New York: HarperSanFrancisco, 1984), 147.
28. Frederick Buechner, *Telling Secrets* (New York: HarperSanFrancisco, 1991), 61.
29. Frederick Buechner, *The Yellow Leaves: A Miscellany* (Louisville: Westminster John Knox Press, 2008), 58.
30. Donald P. Smith, *Empowering Ministry: Ways to Grow in Effectiveness* (Louisville: Westminster John Knox Press, 1996), 57.
31. Mayne, *A Year Lost and Found*, 14.
32. Ibid.
33. Buechner, *The Yellow Leaves: A Miscellany*, 21.
34. Mayne, *A Year Lost and Found*, 14.
35. Ibid., 42.
36. Ibid., 15.
37. Ibid., 28.
38. Ibid., 38.
39. Ibid., 47.
40. Ibid., 50.
41. Ibid.
42. Ibid., 57.

43. John Austin Baker, *The Foolishness of God* (London: Darton, Longman and Todd, 1970), 408.

44. Alister McGrath, *What Was God Doing on the Cross?* (Grand Rapids: Zondervan Publishing House, 1992), 117.

45. Ibid.

46. Ibid.

47. Peter Gomes, *The Good Book: Reading the Bible with Mind and Heart* (New York: William Morrow and Company, Inc., 1996), 229.

48. Mark Oakley, *The Collage of God* (London: Darton, Longman and Todd, 2001), 27.

49. Mayne, *A Year Lost and Found*, 71.

50. Ibid.

51. Ibid.

52. Mayne, "M. E. (Chronic Fatigue Syndrome)," 2.

53. John O'Donohue, *Eternal Echoes: Exploring Our Yearning to Belong* (New York: Cliff Street Books, 1999), 172.

54. Hugh Evan Hopkins, *Charles Simeon of Cambridge* (Grand Rapids: William B. Eerdmans Publishing Company, 1977), 205.

CHAPTER TWO

THIS SUNRISE OF WONDER

Michael Mayne could not have imagined the response to *A Year Lost and Found*. That slim, deeply personal book of reflections on his experience of and his lessons learned from a year's battle with ME struck a chord with readers who both admired and who could relate to Mayne's openness regarding his struggles and doubts amid his 'dark night of the soul.' His next book, *This Sunrise of Wonder,* is larger in scope. Curiously, one can find bibliographic references to three different subtitles for *This Sunrise of Wonder.* The subtitle on the cover of the 1995 Fount (HarperCollins) edition is *Letters for the Journey.* On the inside title page, however, the subtitle reads, *Letters to my grandchildren.* Additionally, one can find references to the subtitle as being *A Quest for God in Art and Nature.* The book was written in a Swiss chalet in the Dolomites during an extended holiday away from London. As the one subtitle makes clear, the book is written in the form of letters to the Maynes' grandchildren. Mayne's premise in writing the book is that its 'letters' provide the kind of guiding principles that will sustain one throughout the journey of life, thus the frequently cited subtitle, *Letters for the Journey.* The guiding principles referred to are largely bits of wisdom Mayne has gleaned from a lifetime of reading and reflection. The book is replete with quotations from and references to a staggering sweep of literature. It is indisputably clear that Mayne was unusually well-read. Readers of his books, particularly in regard to those written after *A Year Lost and Found,* have pondered what sort of filing system Mayne must have employed to keep track of so many sources. Mayne did keep files containing various clippings and hand-written notes, but on the whole his 'filing system' seems to have been based on his memory. His personal library is extensive to say the least, and the books evince his markings of passages of interest. Alison Mayne remembers that on the trip to the chalet where *This Sunrise of Wonder* was written the car was so loaded down with books that there was barely room for the luggage!

Eleven years after it was first published *This Sunrise of Wonder* had sold over 11,500 copies. A new edition was issued in 2008 by Darton, Longman and Todd.

In his review for the *Evening Standard,* A. N. Wilson writes that, "If more Christians had Michael Mayne's gentleness and intelligence, the churches would be fuller."[1] He regards *This Sunrise of Wonder* as a "generous, life-enhancing book, to cherish and to keep."[2] John Barton, in his obituary for Mayne states regarding *This Sunrise of Wonder*, "It is a rich anthology of literature and descriptions of art and music matched by his own mellifluent prose...."[3] John Garton, writing in the *Ripon College Cuddesdon Newsletter* enthuses, "It is guaranteed to stimulate even the most prosaic minds. Time and again there are flashes of perception which will help us to see ourselves and the world in a new light."[4] Ruth Etchells reviewed the book for *Theology*, regarding the piece as "a beautiful book, the sort of book Thomas Traherne might have written if writing today...."[5] She continues, "Certainly it is a book to keep by one for future refocusing when the eyes of our spirit grow misted or clouded over."[6] Writing for *Catholic Herald*, Bernard Green refers to the book as one of "great wisdom."[7] He notes, "In every chapter, I was presented with fresh vistas, new writers and the challenge to go and read more."[8] In Green's view, "Even the most jaded reader could not remain untouched by the feeling of wonder and joy that the book inspires."[9] Michael Marshall, reviewing the book for *The Church of England Newspaper*, writes, "The book is a sheer delight from start to finish as scales fall from the readers' eyes and as literature, poetry, art and music yield up their illusive transcendent capacity to evoke wonder, love and praise."[10] He regards *This Sunrise of Wonder* as "a timely, challenging and very beautiful book to refresh the spirit...."[11] Elizabeth Vardaman notes that she is "astonished by the intensity of the writing, the proliferation of references to vast sources, and the scope of the project."[12] Writing in *Third Way*, Graham McFarlane states, "Mayne offers us hope that amidst the dark colours of life there is still to be found brilliant hues which feed our sense of wonder at the fact that we simply are."[13] In his review for the *Elizabethan Newsletter* Richard Ballard writes, "The voice is an Anglican voice in the best sense: experienced, inclusive, affirming, wholesome, life-enhancing."[14] He adds, "You can't read a book like this only once."[15]

A noted author wrote to Mayne, "I am amazed at the breadth and depth of your reading, and at the facility with which you manage to recall so many apposite references and citations and then weave them deftly into the beautiful fabric of your prose." Another reader writes, "I offer you my sincerest thanks, which seem poor return for what you have given to me." Another appreciative reader observes, *"This Sunrise of Wonder* would be a desert island book."

* * *

The foreword to *This Sunrise of Wonder* is written by Ronald Blythe. He sets the stage for what follows by noting, "What a disaster to pass through our one and only earthly life and to miss its glories."[16] He points out that the book is in no way naively optimistic, but that given life's undeniable disappointments and heartaches there is, at the same time, so much for which to be deeply grateful.[17]

In the book's first chapter Mayne mentions his father in very compassionate terms, recognizing that his father must have known deep pain and anguish to have taken his own life in such a desperate way. He writes, "He must have known a lot about pain and anguish secretly borne, for one day in May he climbed the church tower in the village where he was rector, threw himself down, and was killed almost instantly." [18] He goes on to say that the book (in the form of letters to his grandchildren) is, above all, about wonder.[19] The book's title comes from G. K. Chesterton's autobiography and Chesterton's line, "The object of the artistic and spiritual life is to dig for this sunrise of wonder."[20]

In the first 'letter' he urges his grandchildren to grow into maturity as broad-minded people, worldly in the very best sense of that term, aware of life's complexities and of the vastly different points of view that are represented in the world. Mayne cautions, "Beliefs that are exclusive are usually wrongheaded and always unattractive."[21] Mayne's comments here remind one of a passage in Rowan Williams' *Anglican Identities*. In offering an overview of the broad sweep of Anglican theology at its best, Williams observes that the best of Anglican theologians know:

That as Christians they live among immensities of meaning, live in the wake of a divine action which defies summary explanation. They take it for granted that the believer is always learning, moving in and out of speech and silence in a continuous wonder and a continuous turning inside-out of mind and feeling.[22]

Similarly, Michael Battle writes:

There must be a plurality of theologies, because we do not all apprehend or respond to the transcendent in exactly the same way, nor can we be expected to express our experience in the same way. And this is no cause for lament. Precisely the opposite – it is a reason for rejoicing because it makes mandatory our need for one another because our partial theologies will of necessity require to be corrected by other more or less partial theologies. It reinforces the motif of inter-dependence which is the inalienable characteristic of the body of Christ.[23]

To recognize a plurality of perspectives does not mean that truth is relativized. Mayne would recognize that truth is to be pursued with all vigor, but that it can be and frequently is hard for we humans to grasp fully. As Mark Oakley puts it in *The Collage of God,* "Truth is not the same thing as the elimination of ambiguity."[24] Oakley goes on to say that theology is one of God's invitations for we humans to listen to one another. He continues, "It [theology] is also God's opportunity of letting us know, in often tantalising ways, that he always lies just beyond our reach, forever ancient and forever new."[25] For Oakley, it is important for Christians to understand that our commitment to truth is as that of "pilgrims" rather than as "arrivals," and that in regard to truth we are first and foremost "explorers" not "illustrators."[26]

Mayne's contention that exclusive claims to truth are usually wrongheaded and always unattractive recalls a passage from John Claypool's *God the Ingenius Alchemist: Transforming Tragedy into Blessing.* Encouraging an open-mindedness in matters of theology rather than exclusivity, he writes, "Realizing that there is more in God than we can ever fully know, we can sense certain aspects of the Mystery and share our witness with each other as honest gifts, rather than sledgehammer absolutes imposed coercively on others."[27]

* * *

In her book, *The Writing Life*, Annie Dillard, in some of the most oft-quoted words of contemporary literature, urges:

> Write as if you were dying. At the same time, assume you write for an audience consisting solely of terminal patients. That is, after all, the case. What would you begin writing if you knew you would die soon? What could you say to a dying person that would not enrage by its triviality?[28]

Mayne cites this passage, suggesting that his desire is to write of things that do not prove trivial, but instead are of lasting value for a life's journey filled with wonder and thanksgiving.[29] For Dillard, this language stems from the period when she was writing her extraordinary book, *Pilgrim at Tinker Creek.* Philip Yancey notes that during the writing of the book Dillard lost a brother-in-law to leukemia. He quotes Dillard, who says that against the background of her loved one's battle with the disease, "I could not write this little cheerful nature book, nor could I write a new version of the argument from design. I had to write for people who are dying or grieving – that's everybody."[30]

* * *

At the end of the first chapter Mayne includes one of the most pivotal passages of the book: "If I could have waved a fairy grandfather's wand at your birth and wished you just one gift it would not have been beauty or riches or a long life: it would have been the gift of wonder."[31]

In Chapter Two of the book, Mayne counsels his readers to embrace the ultimate mystery that is God. The mystery surrounding our Creator is to be embraced, not denied. Mayne writes that a mystery in the religious sense is not something to be figured out through human logic or cleverness, noting, "A mystery in the religious, as opposed to the P. D. James sense, is not some truth that can be fully understood once the wit and cunning of our brains have fathomed it out."[32] Our worship of God is an acknowledgment of God's 'Otherness.' Mayne's friend, Basil Hume, writes in *The Mystery of the Cross*, quoting an unnamed Greek Orthodox theologian, "We see that it is not the task of Christianity to provide easy answers to every question, but to make us progressively aware of a mystery. God is not so much the object of our

knowledge as the cause of our wonder."[33] In *The Mystery of Love*, Hume states
that a mystery:

> Is a reality which we can never understand, nor even discover for ourselves.
> This mystery can never be solved. It can only be entered and explored by one
> who accepts with awe and reverence that the deepest reality is unimaginably
> greater than we can ever comprehend....[34]

Hume concludes the passage: "Beyond the limitations of our senses, and even
the horizon of death, lies a place of inexpressible joy, the foundation of all life
and love."[35]

Throughout *This Sunrise of Wonder* Mayne is keen to encourage
readers to relish the wonders of creation, and not to take any moment or sight for
granted. In *The Wounded Healer: Ministry in Contemporary Society,* Henri
Nouwen reminds us of Teilhard de Chardin's dictum, "To him who can see,
nothing is profane."[36] One of the realities we must learn to 'see' is our own
uniqueness as individual children of God. Mayne writes that one of the most
"Godlike" characteristics we can acquire is a comfort with our own being, a
contentedness in being oneself, "For there is a still centre at the very deepest
part of you where you are yourself without subtraction. But it is a sacred place,
and sacred places are a little scary."[37] Mayne would have his readers to be free
of anxiety regarding their own validity in the eyes of God. In a related passage,
Rowan Williams refers in his *Where God Happens: Discovering Christ in One
Another*, to "the peaceful worthwhileness of each person."[38] Along with
Williams, Mayne would have his readers to be at peace with themselves,
comfortable in their own skin as God's beloved children, contented with who
and where they are at any given point in life. Williams suggests in his book,
Christ on Trial: How the Gospel Unsettles Our Judgement, "Arrive. The
hardest thing in the world, they say, is to be where you are."[39]

In addition to being a close friend, Mayne was enormously appreciative
of Frederick Buechner's writings. On page 55 of *This Sunrise of Wonder* Mayne
cites the passage from Buechner's *Now and Then* which includes the oft-quoted
phrase, "Listen to your life." The passage reads in full:

> Listen to your life. See it for the fathomless mystery that it is. In the boredom
> and pain of it no less than in the excitement and gladness; touch, taste, smell
> your way to the heavenly and hidden heart of it because in the last analysis all
> moments are key moments, and life itself is grace.[40]

Given his experience with ME, Mayne surely embraced as heartily as is possible
the truth that all moments are indeed key, to be valued and cherished as such. In
A Room Called Remember: Uncollected Pieces, Frederick Buechner writes,
"You are alive. That's all that matters, and the sheer wonder and grace of it are
staggering, the sense of life as gift, and the sense of the pricelessness of each
moment too, even the most humdrum."[41] Relatedly, in *Secrets in the Dark: A
Life in Sermons,* Buechner urges, "Pay attention. As a summation of all that I

have had to say as a writer, I would settle for that."[42] In *Bird by Bird: Some Instructions on Writing and Life*, Anne Lamott states, "There is ecstasy in paying attention."[43]

Beginning in *A Year Lost and Found* and running through to his last book, *The Enduring Melody*, Mayne addresses thoroughly and compellingly the importance of learning to live and be content in the present moment. His passion for 'the present' reminds one of a passage from Anne Lamott's aforementioned book. The title, *Bird by Bird: Some Instructions on Writing and Life*, comes from a moment in the life of her young son, Sam. Overwhelmed by a school project on birds, Sam was so daunted by the project that he was having trouble even getting started. Sam's grandfather counseled his young grandson wisely. "Bird by bird, Buddy. Just take it bird by bird."[44]

Richard John Neuhaus chronicles his experience of a close brush with death and his eventual recovery in *As I Lay Dying: Meditations Upon Returning*. He observes poignantly, "Having never stopped to live in the present moment, we one day run out of present moments and discover we have not lived at all."[45] He continues, "It is true in every present moment: You have all the time there is."[46] In *Pilgrim at Tinker Creek* Annie Dillard puts it: "*Spend* the afternoon. You can't take it with you."[47] Randy Pausch, author of the runaway bestseller, *The Last Lecture*, cautions, "Time is all you have. And you may find one day that you have less time than you think."[48] Sam Keen warns us in *Learning to Fly: Reflections on Fear, Trust, and the Joy of Letting Go,* "Focusing on a distant goal, we never cherish the moment. We mortgage the present to make a down payment on a future that keeps receding."[49]

* * *

Daniel Hallock has written a slim book titled, *Six Months to Live: Learning from a Young Man with Cancer*. The book chronicles the tragic death of Matt Gauger, who died of cancer as a newly-married young man after a courageous battle against the disease. Hallock writes of Matt and his young wife Cynthia cherishing each moment they had together during his illness prior to his death. Cynthia Gauger remembers hauntingly, "There was no time to be inwardly asleep."[50]

* * *

Throughout *This Sunrise of Wonder* Mayne praises God as Creator, and praises the beauty and wonder of creation. He is quite clear in pointing out that God does not, however, equate to nature. Mayne is no pantheist. Creation is a wondrous sign of the presence and reality of God but is not in and of itself divine, as God "is the condition and ground of all that exists, expressed in, but not limited by, the natural world."[51] In Mayne's understanding, "The whole world is sacramental and the whole creation marked with the signature of its Creator, and...the only way to find the holy is in the ordinary...the ordinary is far more extraordinary than we think."[52]   Of course, key to this theological understanding is the reality that God has come to us in 'ordinary' life in the person of Jesus and has made the love of God fully known.

Mayne goes to great lengths in the book to discuss the reality of our "astonishing" universe.[53]   Key to maintaining awareness of the wonder of creation is a childlike appreciation of the beauty of the world. In his view, one of the most profound as well as challenging sayings of Jesus is that news of the kingdom is to be received as little children. Mayne is clear that here Jesus does not mean childish, as in selfish and temperamental, but childlike, with a fresh awareness of the world. He writes, "It is as if we need to be born anew into a fresh awareness of the world and of each other if we are to find our fulfillment together in what he called 'The Kingdom of God.'"[54] For mature adults, the first innocence of childhood is gone, but a mature adult is nonetheless able to choose to remember to see the world with eyes of wonder and to experience life in a spirit of gratitude.[55] Mayne cautions that when we lose our sense of wonder, the mystery of the holy is diminished, and when our sense of holiness recedes, the sacredness of human life becomes "cheap."[56] Mayne links our capacity for wonder with our capacity for compassion, noting, "Wonder and compassion go hand-in-hand."[57] Importantly, he argues that compassion begins with oneself, seeing oneself as beloved in the eyes of God. He asserts, "It is a kind of blasphemy to view ourselves with so little compassion when God views us with so much."[58]

* * *

Undergirding the theology running through *This Sunrise of Wonder* is the foundational Christian assumption that God is a God of love and that God's love for humanity can be trusted. In order to trust God, a person must come to have faith in the bedrock reality of God's love, for, "We need to know whether we can walk through this world as those who, in some amazing way, are not only 'fearfully and wonderfully made', but also loved."[59] In the latter portion of the book Mayne states that the two most crucial things for a follower of Jesus Christ to learn are what it means to trust and what it means to love.[60] This sentiment is echoed in Rowan Williams' book, *Tokens of Trust: An Introduction to Christian Beliefs*. There Williams states succinctly, "Christian belief is really about knowing who and what to trust."[61] Williams describes faith as "moving deeper into trust as we discover what it means to be the object of an eternally trustworthy love."[62] Similarly, in *The Real God: A Response to Anthony Freeman's God in Us*, Richard Harries writes, "I believe that when I pray to God…what I mean is essentially what Jesus meant, namely that there is a wise and loving power behind human existence, whom I can trust utterly."[63] Barbara Brown Taylor, in her *Leaving Church: A Memoir of Faith,* says that faith has "far more to do with trust than with certainty."[64] A crucial part of the wonder Mayne encourages in his readers is grounded in an abiding belief in the trustworthiness of the love of God. Mayne wishes for his grandchildren, and for

18 *This Sunrise of Wonder*

every child of God, even amid the undeniable difficulties life brings, "A way of being and a frame of mind that is trusting rather than anxious, grateful rather than grudging, compassionate rather than judgemental, and outgoing rather than selfish."[65]

Notes

1. A. N. Wilson, "Marvels of Faith," *Evening Standard,* 30 January 1995, 24.
2. Ibid.
3. John Barton, Obituary for Michael Mayne, *The Church of England Newspaper*, 28.
4. John Garton, review of *This Sunrise of Wonder*, by Michael Mayne, *Ripon College Cuddesdon Newsletter*, 1996, 24.
5. Ruth Etchells, review of *This Sunrise of Wonder*, by Michael Mayne, *Theology* 99 (March/April 1996): 168.
6. Ibid.
7. Bernard Green, "Westminster's Dean Takes Spiritual Stock," *Catholic Herald* 10 (March 1995): 6.
8. Ibid.
9. Ibid.
10. Michael Marshall, "Recovering a Sense of Wonder of Being Human," *The Church of England Newspaper,* 31 March 1995, 10.
11. Ibid.
12. Elizabeth Vardaman, Personal correspondence.
13. Graham McFarlane, review of *This Sunrise of Wonder*, by Michael Mayne, *Third Way*, March 1995, 30.
14. Richard Ballard, review of *This Sunrise of Wonder*, by Michael Mayne, *Elizabethan Newsletter,* Election Term 1995, 2.
15. Ibid.
16. Michael Mayne, *This Sunrise of Wonder* (London: Fount, 1995), x.
17. Ibid., xi.
18. Ibid., 5.
19. Ibid., 7.
20. Ibid.
21. Ibid., 9.
22. Rowan Williams, *Anglican Identities* (Cambridge, MA: Cowley Publications, 2003), 7.
23. Michael Battle, *Reconciliation: The Ubuntu Theology of Desmond Tutu* (Cleveland, OH: The Pilgrim Press, 1997), 33.
24. Mark Oakley, *The Collage of God*, 8.
25. Ibid., 10.
26. Ibid., 62.
27. John R. Claypool, *God the Ingenius Alchemist: Transforming Tragedy into Blessing* (Harrisburg, PA: Morehouse Publishing, 2005), xvii.
28. Annie Dillard, *The Writing Life* (New York: HarperPerennial, 1990), 68.
29. Mayne, *This Sunrise of Wonder*, 9.
30. Philip Yancey, *Soul Survivor: How Thirteen Unlikely Mentors Helped My Faith Survive the Church* (New York: Doubleday, 2003), 233.

31. Mayne, *This Sunrise of Wonder*, 11.

32. Ibid., 17.

33. Basil Hume, *The Mystery of the Cross* (Brewster, MA: Paraclete Press, 1998), 5.

34. Basil Hume, *The Mystery of Love* (London: Darton, Longman and Todd, 2000), 2.

35. Ibid.

36. Henri Nouwen, *The Wounded Healer: Ministry in Contemporary Society* (New York: Image Books, 1979), 46.

37. Mayne, *This Sunrise of Wonder*, 24.

38. Rowan Williams, *Where God Happens: Discovering Christ in One Another* (Boston: New Seeds, 2005), xii.

39. Rowan Williams, *Christ on Trial: How the Gospel Unsettles Our Judgement* (Grand Rapids: William B. Eerdmans Publishing Company, 2000), 21.

40. Frederick Buechner, *Now and Then* (New York: HarperSanFrancisco, 1983), 87.

41. Frederick Buechner, *A Room Called Remember: Uncollected Pieces,* 185.

42. Frederick Buechner, *Secrets in the Dark: A Life in Sermons* (New York: HarperSanFrancisco, 2006), 183.

43. Anne Lamott, *Bird by Bird: Some Instructions on Writing and Life* (New York: Anchor Books, 1994), 100.

44. Ibid., 19.

45. Richard John Neuhaus, *As I Lay Dying: Meditations Upon Returning* (New York: Basic Books, 2002), 66.

46. Ibid.

47. Annie Dillard, *Pilgrim at Tinker Creek* (New York: Perennial Classics, 1974), 274.

48. Randy Pausch and Jeffrey Zaslow, *The Last Lecture* (London: Hodder & Stoughton, 2008), 111.

49. Sam Keen, *Learning to Fly: Reflections on Fear, Trust, and the Joy of Letting Go* (New York: Broadway Books, 1999), 236.

50. Daniel Hallock, *Six Months to Live: Learning from a Young Man with Cancer* (Farmington, PA: The Plough Publishing House, 2001), 117.

51. Mayne, *This Sunrise of Wonder*, 63.

52. Ibid., 72.

53. Ibid., 121.

54. Ibid., 130.

55. Ibid., 131.

56. Ibid., 235.

57. Ibid.

58. Ibid., 248.

59. Ibid., 80.

60. Ibid., 295.

61. Rowan Williams, *Tokens of Trust: An Introduction to Christian Beliefs* (Louisville: Westminster John Knox Press, 2007), viii.

62. Ibid., 158.

63. Richard Harries, *The Real God: A Response to Anthony Freeman's God in Us* (London: Mowbray, 1994), 33.

64. Barbara Brown Taylor, *Leaving Church: A Memoir of Faith* (New York: HarperSanFrancisco, 2006), 170.

65. Mayne, *This Sunrise of Wonder*, 296.

CHAPTER THREE

PRAY, LOVE, REMEMBER

"It is pure gold, and will surely fire any Christian's intellect, emotion, and will."[1] Thus writes Michael Perry in *Church Times* of *Pray, Love, Remember*, the first book written by Michael Mayne after his retirement from Westminster in 1996. *Pray, Love, Remember* is a kind of 'love letter' to the people with whom he worked for ten years, as well as to the institution itself which he served with dedication and effectiveness. The volume is a Lent book, but its usefulness is in no way limited to that liturgical season. The back cover of the book reads in part, "It is a personal account by the former Dean of Westminster of the varied and largely unknown life and ministry of Westminster Abbey, with reflections on the Christian story and what it means to be human."

Other than *A Year Lost and Found*, this is the smallest of Mayne's major works but it is chock-full of content. Chronologically it is sandwiched between two of Mayne's larger, and his two most similar pieces, *This Sunrise of Wonder* and *Learning to Dance*. *Pray, Love, Remember* is different, a distinct work in Mayne's corpus. Among his five major works *Pray, Love, Remember* is Mayne's least well-known book, though having sold upwards of 8,000 copies in ten years its readership is more than respectable.

In a review for the *Newsletter of St. Paul's Knightsbridge*, Ysenda Maxton Graham regards the book as "so illuminating and comforting that it makes one wish there could be a Michael Mayne hotline to ring up at times of tragedy."[2] In *Church Times*, Debbie Thrower writes, "The book is part diary, part reminiscence, and part a study that explains to us the Christian story, and what it is to be human."[3] The reviewer for the *Westminster Abbey Chorister* holds that Michael Mayne "once more reveals his sensitivity, humility and compassion in a way which is both self-effacing and unselfconscious."[4] The reviewer adds, "It is a devotional book, a gentle yet stimulating spiritual guide, finely wrought, deeply absorbing and eminently satisfying."[5]

In his brief overview of the book, Peter Eaton suggests that "anyone who plans to visit Westminster Abbey should have *Pray, Love, Remember* as a guide."[6] This is a perceptive observation. The book is a rich resource on the abbey's history and its ministry in contemporary British society. Not only for visitors, those who are on staff or who volunteer at the abbey would do well to know the contents of *Pray, Love, Remember*. There is no other resource like it.

One of the appreciative readers who corresponded with Mayne regarding the book urges, "I hope that you are enjoying your retirement but please don't stop writing!"

The foreword to *Pray, Love, Remember* is by Alan Bennett. He praises the literary quality of the book and joins the chorus of Mayne's readers who are deeply impressed by the breadth of his reading.[7] Bennett graciously notes that Mayne's very considerable learning is worn lightly.[8] For Bennett, the actual form of the book – part diary, part reminiscence, part devotional instruction – makes for a "wonderfully readable mixture."[9]   He observes that Mayne's willingness to be vulnerable and approachable, evinced in *A Year Lost and Found*, is also characteristic of this new book.

In introducing *Pray, Love, Remember*, Mayne allows that it is a very personal book: "In my view, the only kind of book really worth reading – about the nature and significance for me of a place that over ten years became such a deeply valued part of my life."[10] As the book proceeds, Mayne offers a kind of tour of the abbey, providing a bit of history and then his personal reflections on the various sections which combine to constitute Westminster Abbey, one of the most recognizable and significant buildings in the world.

In this book, Mayne addresses the subject of sin directly for one of the very few times in all of his five major works (approximately 1,000 pages of text). In the vast majority of his work, Mayne puts the focus squarely on grace. His books convey unmistakably clearly God's love, God's compassion, God's mercy; and Mayne's theological emphasis is unabashedly on humanity's reconciliation with God through grace rather than its alienation from God through sin. In *Pray, Love, Remember*, as in the writings of the sixth-century historian, Evagrius, sin is described as the forgetfulness of God's goodness.[11] A part of our forgetfulness, in Mayne's view, is our refusal as human beings to become the people we truly are in God's love.[12] For Mayne sin is:

> To settle for less than I might be. To choose the lesser good. To lack curiosity
> and wonder. To miss the mark [the most literal definition of the word for sin in
> the New Testament] because my sights are fixed too low. Not to perceive that I
> am 'fearfully and wonderfully made' in God's image.[13]

Mayne concludes the passage, "When I ask God to forgive me, I do so because in settling for less than I am created to be, I know not what I do."[14]

This book on Westminster Abbey includes, fittingly, consideration of church architecture, and in particular, medieval, gothic understandings of sacred space. Mayne affirms the vision of those who planned and built spaces such as the abbey, for, "Those who built our churches created spaces intended to arouse in those who entered them a sense of entering a special place, evoking that sense of awe which is the beginning of worship."[15] Here one gets a clear impression of Mayne's presupposition that worship of God does in fact begin with a sense of awe – not a sense of God's separation from humanity – but God's 'Otherness.' Mayne contributed a chapter to *Coventry's First Cathedral: The*

Cathedral and Priory of St. Mary. The book is a collection of papers from the 1993 symposium celebrating the 950th anniversary of cathedral ministry in Coventry. In his contribution Mayne states explicitly, "To feel awe is to begin to worship."[16] He says further:

> This is why the great monastic abbeys and churches were built: in order that the worship of God, the singing of the psalms, the reading of the scriptures and the celebrating of the Eucharist, might be done not just with awe and devotion, but aided by all the richness of the architecture, all the subtlety of colour and ceremonial, all the beauty of words and music, of which we human beings are when we approach God – or rather, when we invite God to approach us.[17]

In the great cathedrals and abbeys:

> By our daily round of prayer and worship, the doing of the *Opus Dei*, we stand with those who affirm night and day that God is worthy of our love and praise, and that every living soul, made in God's likeness, is of infinite value in his sight.[18]

When Mayne assumed the Deanery of Westminster, it was his foundational assumption that meaningful Christian worship must be at the very center of the abbey's life, that the abbey must be and indeed *feel* like a church, instead of it being experienced primarily as a great national shrine and tourist attraction. In speaking of the daily round of services offered in the cathedrals and abbeys of the Church of England, Mayne holds, "All are part of the *Opus Dei*, and everything else we do is secondary."[19] As Dean of Westminster, Mayne was all too familiar with the enormous costs of maintaining a massive medieval building. Still, in his view such buildings have their place in the life of the church as centers of truly awe-inspiring worship.

Of course, Mayne was comfortable with the fact that the vast majority of Christian worship does not take place in the grandeur of a massive stone cathedral or abbey. Delightfully, in his remarks at the Bowen conference in 1996 he recalls a time in Texas when for an outdoor eucharist wine was available in abundance but the only 'bread' available was gold colored, goldfish-shaped cocktail biscuits!

Mayne did not author many published book reviews, but he did write a review of the important book, *Embracing the Chaos: Theological Responses to AIDS*, edited by James Woodward. The review appears in *Theology*. In the review Mayne makes clear that while churches are first and foremost places of worship, at the same time they are to be places where "people may share their vulnerability and find healing, places of openness and love...."[20] He notes poignantly:

> Those of us who have been privileged to witness the AIDS support groups that have burgeoned in our larger cities [largely in non-church settings at the time of

the review in 1990] cannot but be moved by (and made ashamed of) the
supportive love, forgiveness and acceptance that are often found there.[21]

In any assessment of the broad sweep of Mayne's years of ministry, it must be
remembered that he was in the forefront of the church's nascent outreach to
those with HIV/AIDS and their carers.

In *Pray, Love, Remember* Mayne revisits the subject of the nature of
faith, covered more thoroughly in *This Sunrise of Wonder.* The reader is
reminded that faith does not imply absolute certainty, but instead a willingness
to explore the mystery of God. A faithful person does not pretend to possess all
the answers but is willing to acknowledge and to live the questions. Similarly to
hope, faith is a mindset, an orientation. Honest doubts are a part of faith, not its
denial, and a person of faith's doubts are but an example of a healthy refusal to
be "prematurely convinced."[22]

Clearly for Mayne, prayer is to be the very lifeblood of the abbey's
ministry. Friends and colleagues of Mayne universally remember him as a
person of prayer. One of his most revealing statements regarding prayer is:

> Prayer is not an escape from life, a few minutes cut out of life, but a regular,
> disciplined reminder that all life is lived in God's presence, a marveling at
> God's love as that is shown in Christ, a thankful responding to that
> transcendent reality by whom we are held in being.[23]

Though obviously extremely well-educated theologically, Mayne did not
consider himself primarily to be a theologian but a pastor. He makes no claim at
any point to being an original thinker in matters of theology. His writings are,
consequently, fundamentally pastoral in nature. He is concerned to write about
the life of prayer rather than to presume to develop 'original' theological ideas.
Here one is reminded of a passage from Mark Oakley where he claims, "A true
Christian liberality will be more concerned to direct our limited language to God
rather than about God."[24]

Mayne's tenure as Dean of Westminster was informed by his
assumption that the abbey's life was to be loyal to its heritage but not
encumbered by it. Mayne makes a distinction between the abbey's inheritance
and its tradition, noting, "I always believed that the Abbey's role, like the
Church's role, is to be loyal to its heritage but not encumbered by it. In short, to
distinguish its inheritance from its tradition."[25] The abbey's inheritance is to be
a vibrant, engaged, relevant and fully functioning church. The author has a
friend who was in St. Paul's Cathedral, London, in the 1980s when a
professional tour guide announced to those in her charge, "This used to be a
church, but is now a museum." Uninformed, and unfair in the extreme, such an
errant view of the abbey would have been a nightmare to Michael Mayne.

It is important to note that while Dean, Mayne did not allow himself to
be consumed solely with administrative duties. He brought a pastoral sensitivity
to Westminster in 1986 and maintained that outlook for the duration of his

tenure. Mayne was available as a counselor. Also, his friend and colleague Anthony Harvey remembers that Mayne "sought to make every employee and every voluntary helper feel needed as part of a caring institution."[26] He kept constantly in mind the view that, "Jesus comes to be the love of God in our midst. That, and nothing less than that, is what every Christian church exists to proclaim...."[27] Thus, for Mayne, pastoral ministry remained uppermost in his sense of vocation.

Mayne revisits briefly in *Pray, Love, Remember* the subject addressed thoroughly in *A Year Lost and Found* of being open and honest regarding one's experiences and of a willingness to admit one's vulnerability. He writes that those who have been most helpful to him in his life's journey are those persons willing to speak or preach or write out of their own experiences and who allow themselves, "At appropriate times, with reticence and hopefully without self-indulgence, to admit and share their own vulnerability."[28] An appropriate reticence about saying too much remained important to Mayne at all times. As a pastoral counselor, however, he understood that someone coming for counseling had to be able to see that the counselor embraced her or his own humanity and could therefore offer compassion and understanding, for, "They will only be attracted to you in the first place if they know from the sort of person you have revealed yourself to be that you are not afraid of sharing your own humanity."[29]

It is in *Pray, Love, Remember* where Mayne writes most fully concerning his father's suicide. He ponders what his father must have been like, recognizing that he is bone of his father's bone and flesh of his father's flesh. He refers to his father as being wounded and admits that he will never know what deep despair led his father to take such a desperate action as suicide, noting, "What he was like, this wounded man whose genes I carry, or what deep unhappiness led him to take such a desperate action, I could only guess."[30] A part of Mayne's remarkable capacity for compassion sprang from his understanding, issuing from his father's suicide, that no one can really ever understand fully what is in the heart and soul of another human being and that one dare not presume to pass ultimate judgment on another's life or death, as this is for God alone.[31] In one of his most poignant passages, Mayne relates that a woman who remembered his father once conveyed, "I was fifteen when he died. He was so popular in the village; and, you know, he was such a jolly man." Mayne observes, "How little we reveal. How little we know."[32] Mark Oakley reminds us of a line from Ian McEwan's novel *Amsterdam:* "We know so little about each other. We lie mostly submerged like ice floes, with our visible social selves projecting only cool and white."[33]

Faith as trust, not as certainty, is a recurring theme for Mayne. This subject is addressed in *Pray, Love, Remember* specifically as it relates to Jesus. Mayne reminds his readers of Jesus' humanity, the incarnational reality that Jesus experienced life as we do and is therefore capable of the ultimate in compassion and understanding. Mayne writes that Jesus' message, ultimately, is, 'Trust me, I give you my word.'[34] This phrase, 'I give you my word', is crucial to Mayne's theology. In one of the meditations he offered at the Bowen conference in 1996, Mayne states that 'I give you my word' is the "essence" of the gospel message. For Mayne, 'the word' can be trusted amid anything that life may bring. Near the end of the book, Mayne notes that when he chose Ophelia's 'Pray, love, remember' from *Hamlet* as the book's title, he did so because these words sum up for him the very essence of the Christian life.[35] In his mature years Mayne understood that what matters most for a Christian is praying, loving and remembering.[36]

NOTES

1. Michael Perry, "Not So Much a Retreat, More of a Challenge," review of *Pray, Love, Remember,* by Michael Mayne, *Church Times,* 29 January 1999, 14.

2. Ysenda Maxton Graham, review of *Pray, Love, Remember,* by Michael Mayne, *Newsletter of St. Paul's Knightsbridge,* February 1999, 8.

3. Debbie Thrower, "What I'm Reading," review of *Pray, Love, Remember,* by Michael Mayne, *Church Times,* 14 October 2005, 24.

4. Review of *Pray, Love, Remember,* by Michael Mayne, *The Westminster Abbey Chorister* 3 (Winter 1998/9): 45.

5. Ibid., 46.

6. Peter Eaton, "A Rich Life: The Writings of Michael Mayne," 19.

7. Michael Mayne, *Pray, Love, Remember* (London: Darton, Longman and Todd, 1998), xii.

8. Ibid., xiii.

9. Ibid.

10. Ibid., xv.

11. Ibid., 3.

12. Ibid., 46.

13. Ibid.

14. Ibid.

15. Ibid., 19.

16. Michael Mayne, "The Celebration of the 950th Anniversary of the Founding of the Church of St. Mary," in *Coventry's First Cathedral: The Cathedral and Priory of St. Mary.* Papers from the 1993 Anniversary Symposium, ed. George Demidowicz (Stamford, England: Paul Watkins, 1994), 191.

17. Ibid.

18. Ibid., 192.

19. Ibid.

20. Michael Mayne, review of *Embracing the Chaos: Theological Responses to AIDS,* ed. James Woodward, *Theology* 93 (September/October 1990): 416.

21. Ibid.

22. Mayne, *Pray, Love, Remember,* 21.

23. Ibid., 24.

24. Mark Oakley, *The Collage of God,* 56.

25. Mayne, *Pray, Love, Remember,* 38.

26. Anthony Harvey, Obituary for Michael Mayne, *The Independent on Sunday,* 2.

27. Mayne, *Pray, Love, Remember,* 49.

28. Ibid., 55.
29. Ibid., 56.
30. Ibid., 57.
31. Ibid., 58.
32. Ibid., 59.
33. Oakley, *The Collage of God*, 60.
34. Mayne, *Pray, Love, Remember*, 74.
35. Ibid., 122.
36. Ibid., 135.

CHAPTER FOUR

LEARNING TO DANCE

Michael Mayne intended that *Pray, Love, Remember* should be his last book. Both in published material and in letters, Mayne expresses his concern about ever being, in his words, "tiresomely repetitive." To Mayne's own satisfaction, he had said what he had to say in *A Year Lost and Found, This Sunrise of Wonder,* and, finally, in *Pray, Love, Remember.* His publisher (Darton, Longman and Todd), however, took a decidedly different point of view and approached Mayne regarding the possibility of another book. At first Mayne demurred. In a letter to his (eventual) editor, Brendan Walsh, Mayne wrote on 21 January 2000, "I'm by nature a hoarder and dispenser of the thoughts of others rather than an original thinker...."[1] Here Mayne is acknowledging his anxiety concerning the prospect of a fourth major book being repetitive. In about a year's time, however, Mayne accepted the fact that there was another book in him. He wrote to Brendan Walsh on 8 January 2001, "The book will be very personal, as I don't know how to write any other way."[2] *Learning to Dance* was published later that year. In Mayne's corpus, the book is most similar to *This Sunrise of Wonder.* While there are numerous points of contact between the two pieces, and indeed, some overlap, *Learning to Dance* is in no way a rehash of *This Sunrise of Wonder* but stands very well on its own. The perspective offered in *Learning to Dance* is even more considered than that of *This Sunrise of Wonder.* Willfully undertaking the project, Mayne clearly did intend for this to be his final book, his 'signing off' from the mature standpoint of a retired clergyman who had offered a lifetime of service to the church. A number of ideas present in *This Sunrise of Wonder* are taken further in *Learning to Dance.* Any reader who appreciates Mayne's first 'big book', *This Sunrise of Wonder*, will find that *Learning to Dance* adds substantively to the former's contents. Some eight years after it first appeared, sales of *Learning to Dance* approach 10,000.

The most notable difference between *Learning to Dance* and *This Sunrise of Wonder* is that the relationship between religion and science is explored in much greater detail in *Learning to Dance.* Mayne's treatment of science, from a lay perspective, calls to mind Annie Dillard's *Pilgrim at Tinker Creek.* In his review praising *Learning to Dance* in *The Salisbury Cathedral News*, John Austin Baker suggests, "Few things are more urgent than that

Christians should lose their fearful distrust of science, and rejoice in it as a major window on to God."[3] Baker notes that alongside his discussion of the wonders of creation, Mayne, as always, honestly explores "the horrors, the suffering [of life]."[4] Baker recognizes that, as a writer, Mayne "has helped and enhanced the lives of thousands...."[5] It is Baker who articulates in print what most of Mayne's readers ponder: "He [Mayne] either has the best stocked mind in England or a unique filing system!"[6] The answer appears to have been the former. In his conclusion Baker opines, "If you buy it, buy two copies, for you will want to lend it, and if you do you will never see that copy again!"[7]

Victor Stock reviewed the book for *Church Times* and writes in response to Mayne's balanced treatment of both life's joys and its sorrows, "To be hopeful while being honest is perhaps the deepest and most miraculous kind of Christianity."[8] He notes, "Michael Mayne is able to write personally, for example, about the suicide of his father, but he does so with a delicacy that will enable others studying this book to take the risk of sharing something of themselves."[9] David Scott, in his review in *The Franciscan,* mentions, "The suicide of the author's father, also a priest, was one of those most desperately unforgettable moments in my lifetime's reading."[10]

In her review for *The Tablet,* Margaret Silf considers *Learning to Dance* to be, "A landmark in the exploration of contemporary spirituality. It crosses boundaries hitherto well policed, and breaks open the packaging in which we too easily try to contain our believing."[11] Similarly to Elizabeth Vardaman's wording regarding *This Sunrise of Wonder,* Silf finds that *Learning to Dance* is "authoritative yet accessible."[12] In her opinion, the book is "The ripe fruit of the dance in the author's own being between a fine intellect and an open heart."[13] To her the book represents "an intricate and fascinating tapestry of interwoven themes."[14] She regards the book as "an important and substantial contribution to an evolving genre of literature."[15] Silf applauds Mayne's carrying forward the argument begun in *This Sunrise of Wonder* that, "Fixing God in 'certainties' leads to exclusive, divisive systems that are the opposite of faith."[16] She concludes, "This is the kind of book – a rare event – that one would happily take away to a desert island."[17]

The review in *Scientific and Medical Network Review* finds the book to be "delightful and erudite."[18] Further, "The writing is conversational but the insights profound and his choice of quotations – especially poetry – is wonderful."[19] Similarly, Mike Starkey, in his review for *Christian Herald,* notes, "The overall effect is like a fireside chat with a genial, well-read churchman, full of wonder at the world around him, and alert to where God may be found in it all."[20] Starkey correctly observes that Mayne frequently "seems more at peace with questions than answers."[21]

Rick Mercer observes in *Church Times,* "It is Mayne at his best, reflecting in retirement on life, science, literature, music, art, heaven, and everything."[22] In Mercer's opinion Mayne makes, "A real contribution to our understanding of the complexities and tensions of our faith."[23] Similarly to John Austin Baker, Mercer notes that Mayne "has an encyclopaedic mind."[24]

Margaret McAllister states in *Church Times*, "As a writer, he [Mayne] takes us by the hand. I never felt out of my depth, but there is much to digest and absorb."[25] She regards the book as one to "keep coming back to."[26] The review in *Parish News* regards the book as a "rich and generous gift."[27] In *Methodist Recorder* Patricia Billsborrow goes so far as to say that, "Every page contains a treasure."[28]

An appreciative reader wrote to Mayne, "What a stunning achievement. It is quite truthfully one of the finest books I have ever read." Similarly, another reader writes, "I do not remember any book I have read in years which has touched me so deeply." Another writes, "It is a treasure-house of delights and profound insights both human and spiritual." Other readers responses include, "I found the mix of poetry and music with physics, biology and maths irresistible. Michael Mayne has a richly stocked mind, and makes this an amazingly wide-ranging argument in favour of the reasonableness of Christianity." Also, "He explores the complications and difficulties of faith in such an honest, open-hearted way, without ever seeming pat, that no one could fail to find it helpful." And, "Michael Mayne has opened up a new world to me."

A reader wrote to Mayne that the book "provides one with another enticing and invigorating summons to wonder." Another reader writes that the book is "fascinating and hugely enjoyable." In a letter to Alison Mayne a reader notes, "I continue to be in awe of Michael's mind and his ability to imbue the page with such a celebratory transcendence." Another grateful reader writes to Michael Mayne that *Learning to Dance* is a "beautiful, thoughtful and inspiring companion."

A bishop in the Church of England wrote Mayne to say, "I think it deserves to be a spiritual classic."

* * *

The foreword is written by Dame Cicely Saunders, recognized as the founder of the modern hospice movement. Cicely Saunders and Michael Mayne were friends, and they worked together for years on issues of mutual concern. Given her years of experience working with terminally ill persons, Saunders, like most hospice workers, recognizes the importance of delight, or appreciating and enjoying those good things in life which a healthy person can so easily take for granted.[29] Saunders writes that the book is "enchanting," its key theme being that the universe is our gift from God and is good and can be trusted.[30] She suggests that 'dancing in the dark' is at the center of "this searching book," recalling Julian of Norwich's query as to how all can be well against the backdrop of life's undeniable heartaches.[31] Saunders assures readers that though the book does address both the joyful and the difficult aspects of life the book is, above all, "full of thanksgiving."[32] She suggests that the book is one to stir its readers to gratitude, as Mayne writes from his mature perspective on his life experiences (not all easy), offering readers encouragement in their own journeys through life.[33]

Titles of books being important to Mayne, early on in the text he writes, "For what is it to learn to dance but to spend a lifetime learning to love?"[34] This is a theme running throughout the piece – the dance of life is a journey of learning that we are loved by God and can, consequently, learn *to* love. Later in the work he writes that, "The secret of learning to dance is learning how to sow the seeds of love."[35] The starting place to be able to do this is recognizing what it means to be loved by God.[36] Mayne recalls words from William Tyndale's "Prologue" to the New Testament where Tyndale counsels that the 'good news' makes one "daunce" for joy.[37]

There are frequent points of contact between Mayne's work and that of Annie Dillard. In *For the Time Being*, Dillard writes, "Dancing is no mere expression; it is an achievement. Rabbi Nachman of Bratslav noticed that if the dancers could persuade a melancholy person to join them, his sadness would lift."[38]

* * *

The theme of living contentedly in the present moment is once again prominent for Mayne. Mayne knew the classic work of Jean-Pierre De Caussade, and in his encouragement to his readers to live in the 'now', Mayne reminds readers of Caussade's understanding that no moment is trivial, as each and every moment of life contains a "divine Kingdom, and heavenly sustenance."[39]

A central component to living in the present is taking the time to see and to notice where one is, and what is all around. This theme from *This Sunrise of Wonder* is carried forward in *Learning to Dance*. One is reminded here of a line from Rich Mathis' *Finding a Grace-Filled Life*: "It seems that grace is often found by moving more slowly...."[40] There is also the Eastern dictum, "Drink your tea slowly."

Learning to Dance picks up and carries forward Mayne's concern in *This Sunrise of Wonder* that we truly live life to the fullest rather than merely exist. Joan Chittister, in her book, *The Gift of Years: Growing Older Gracefully*, laments that so often, "We take the gift of life and return it unopened."[41] Mayne would have his readers to open up this gift of God which we call life and explore it in all its richness.

Early on Mayne states that a significant number of people turn to him either in person or by letter in response both to his book recounting his battle with ME and the reality of his father's suicide. His experience of so many people being helped by his books encourages him to offer another work, as always, though, with "proper reticence and restraint."[42] He writes that in learning to dance, in exploring life to the fullest, what most persons are really looking for is what we call home.[43]

* * *

Having written about his father's suicide most fully in *Pray, Love, Remember,* Mayne now turns to his relationship with his mother, who lived to an advanced age.   He explores the frequent complexity of very close relationships from the perspective of his relationship with his mother.   Mayne clearly loved his mother very deeply, but because of her emotional demands upon him he admits that his love for her was often mixed with anger and resentment.   Mayne goes on to convey how, over time, his feelings of resentment were replaced by compassion and forgiveness.[44]   He notes the irony that frequently a person is more comfortable in offering kindness, patience, and forbearance to friends or even strangers than to members of one's own family. He cautions that difficulties in parent/child relationships are rarely one-sided and that the power of forgiveness is nowhere more "potent" than in relationships within one's own immediate family.   Poignantly, Mayne contends that understanding, forgiveness and reconciliation can happen even after a loved one has died as the survivor honestly both seeks and receives forgiveness. Regarding a parent/child relationship, he observes, "Sometimes only in retrospect do you master the movements of this most complicated dance."[45]

* * *

One of the challenges for many people in modern life is the frantic pace of activities which seems to be part and parcel of Western life, particularly in more urban areas.   While Dean of Westminster, Mayne wrestled with the need for 'stillness' amid the whirl of activities in central London.   Retirement in Salisbury juxtaposed against ministry in London helps Mayne to reflect deeply on the essential element of a balance in life between activity and stillness.   He writes that a life with no place for stillness may need some "hard pruning" if it is to have, using a metaphor from nature, a proper shape.[46]

* * *

The subject of creation, and the relationship between science and religion, a significant part of *This Sunrise of Wonder,* receives even more considered attention in *Learning to Dance.*   Mayne writes confidently that scientific progress is no threat to Christianity but rather adds grist to the mill of our theological discussions.   While no threat to the ultimate foundation of faith, progress in science does, however, force thoughtful Christians to reconsider certain aspects of a traditional, at times "immature" concept of God in light of scientific discoveries. Using the example of Darwinism, what such thinking destroyed in Mayne's view is not Christianity, but eighteenth-century Deism.[47] Much of the text of *Learning to Dance* is occupied with Mayne's writing on science and religion from a deeply thoughtful lay (with regard to the science) perspective.   For Mayne, honest scientific inquiry and its results only add to the glorious mystery that is God.

The thinking underlying this discussion in *Learning to Dance* is echoed by Rowan Williams in his book *Tokens of Trust: An Introduction to Christian Beliefs,* wherein he addresses "the pointless stand-off between science and religion."[48] The archbishop writes:

> Faith doesn't try and give an alternative theory about the mechanics of the world; it invites you to take a step further, beyond the nuts and bolts, even beyond the Big Bang, to imagine an activity so unrestricted, so supremely itself, that it depends on nothing and is constantly pouring itself out so that the reality we know depends on it. Creation isn't a theory about how things started; as St. Thomas Aquinas said, it's a way of seeing everything in relation to God. Whatever you encounter is there because God chose that it should be there.[49]

Writing in a similar register as Mayne, Annie Dillard suggests hauntingly in *For the Time Being*, "There are maybe nine galaxies for each of us...."[50]

The wonders and complexities of creation, the evolving advances in the sciences, and the undeniable ambiguities of human existence lead Mayne to a healthy humility regarding the claims of systematic theology. In light of this humility, Mayne is completely secure in the fact that he himself in no way presumes to be writing 'original' theology. An important quotation which helps to inform Mayne's perspective here is from Ludwig Wittgenstein's *Tractatus Logico-Philosophicus* (1922). For Mayne, when all the "dusty theological words" come to their end, we are left with Wittgenstein's maxim, 'Whereof one cannot speak, therein one must remain silent.'[51] In *Anglican Identities* Rowan Williams puts it, "Since God as object is inexhaustible, the grounding of divine will in divine nature reinforces the awareness of the provisionality or inadequacy of what we say and do in respect of God."[52]

Mayne would agree wholeheartedly with Hugh Montefiore, one of his predecessors at Great St. Mary's, Cambridge, when Montefiore writes, "All our dogmas are partial and our doctrines provisional. It is not by these but by our prayers and our life that we make our ultimate affirmations about God, creator, redeemer and sanctifier."[53] In his *Why I Believe in a Personal God: The Credibility of Faith in a Doubting Culture*, George Carey reminds readers of the insight of the anonymous medieval mystic author of *The Cloud of Unknowing*, 'By love he may be caught but by thinking never.'[54]

In *The Collage of God*, Mark Oakley cautions that systematic theology, however sophisticated and "fine-tuned," is "always inevitably historically conditioned...."[55] In *Honest to God*, Mayne's friend and colleague John A. T. Robinson asserts, "I have never really doubted the fundamental truth of the Christian faith – though I have constantly found myself questioning its expression."[56] In his contribution to the collection of essays titled *Michael Ramsey as Theologian*, George Carey studies Ramsey's reaction to Robinson's 'radical' runaway bestselling book. In his analysis Carey writes, "A living faith can never be static. The faith 'once delivered to the saints' has to be appropriated and proclaimed afresh in each generation."[57]

One of Mayne's clear concerns in *Learning to Dance* is to carry forward to its final form his contention that honest, sometimes painful doubts are an essential part of a true faith journey and are not a threat to such a journey. Ironically, it is Mayne's view that doubt is actually a sign of faith. The strength of one's bedrock faith allows one to have doubts which challenge but ultimately do not destroy one's core beliefs. In a similar vein Basil Hume writes in *The Mystery of the Incarnation,* "Remember it is the refusal to believe that hurts him, not the struggle to do so."[58] In a talk for BBC Radio John A. T. Robinson asserts, "Only the man who knows he cannot lose what the Sabbath stands for can afford to criticise it radically. Faith alone can dare to doubt – to the depths."[59]

At times 'not knowing' is simply a reality, and Mayne encourages readers to acknowledge with humility that we do indeed see through a glass darkly. In his collection of essays, *Hints and Guesses II*, George Connor recalls his memory of Thorne Sparkman, sometime Rector of St. Paul's Episcopal Church in Chattanooga, Tennessee, frequently responding to questions of some imponderable, unanswerable nature by saying, "I am so grateful that the Lord has not put me in charge of that." Connor goes on to note, "Would that this attitude were more widespread in Christendom!"[60]

Mark Oakley reminds his readers in *The Collage of God,* "We do well to learn from the mother whale as she warned her baby whale: 'Be careful, my dear, for it is when you are spouting that you are most likely to get harpooned.'"[61]

* * *

Learning to Dance addresses a subject that was obviously important to Mayne and which appears at various points in his writings – his keen desire to confront the reality of the absolute uniqueness of the individual, and that regardless of how much one is loved, even by a spouse, children, or close friends – no human being fully understands another. He writes, "Ultimately, of course, each of us is alone, for that is the flip side of our uniqueness, our wonderfully distinctive selves: What I experience is *my* birth, *my* feelings, *my* sickness, *my* solitude and suffering and dying."[62] And later in the book: "There is, deep within us, a private place, and not even the one who loves me most will ever know exactly what it feels like to be me."[63] Henri Nouwen offers a similar thought in *Beloved: Henri Nouwen in Conversation,* when he says, "You are alone – that's a reality – there's nobody like you around. In a deep, deep way you are alone in the world."[64] One suspects that the point of origin of this emphasis in Mayne's writing stems from his lifetime of reflection on his father's suicide, and how a person so well thought of in the village where he served as priest could, in his own private, internal world, be so despairing that he would take his own life, leaving a wife and a young child aged three behind.

Wrestling with this reality of our ultimate aloneness leads one back to the importance of self-acceptance at a very deep level. Mayne deals with this most fully in *This Sunrise of Wonder*, but it is also present in *Learning to Dance*. George Connor argues regarding a healthy self-acceptance:

> At its best and most enlightened, this is...what the Christian faith does; it allows and encourages us to be ourselves, to develop the talents God has given us, to enjoy the world that He has made, to find the crown and focus of our identity in our worship of Him.[65]

In line with Connor's point, Mayne's urging his readers toward a healthy self-regard is grounded theologically in God's love and grace.

Accepting love and embracing such love for ourselves is one of the great challenges of life. Mayne recognizes the struggle we experience of believing that we are lovable – truly lovable – in God's eyes. In one of the most searching passages in all of contemporary spiritual literature, Annie Dillard writes in *Teaching a Stone to Talk: Expeditions and Encounters,* "For you [God] meant only love, and love, and I felt only fear, and pain. So once in Israel love came to us incarnate, stood in the doorway between two worlds, and we were all afraid."[66]

* * *

While Mayne's focus remains predominantly on God's grace and mercy, he does discuss sin in *Learning to Dance*. Here he refers to Simone Weil's contention that sin, importantly, is not a distance from God, but is instead a turning of our gaze in the wrong direction.[67] He acknowledges that forgiveness is "a complex and often painfully hard process."[68] This is so whether one is struggling with one's own sin or with having been injured by another. He notes that if forgiveness was not difficult, then it would not have the power to be life-changing.[69] Forgiveness for Christians leads to Jesus himself, the embodiment of God's all-forgiving, compassionate love. In Mayne's view, "Forgiveness is a radically changed attitude to life and to others, one that looks not to the past but to the future. It means, for Christians, Jesus of Nazareth."[70] For Mayne, we "join the dance" when we repent, and *trust* in God's mercy, and a new beginning.[71]

* * *

In *The Gift of Years: Growing Older Gracefully*, Joan Chittister writes, "In youth we learn, Marie von Ebner-Eschenbach wrote when she was seventy-five years old, in age we understand."[72] *Learning to Dance* is indeed a generous sharing by Michael Mayne of his lifetime of lessons learned, some of them painful. He observes wisely, "Our faith evolves. It shifts and subtly changes as we change: how I saw life at twenty is not how I see it at seventy-plus."[73] He reflects in maturity:

With an increasingly limited time ahead, I think of those places I shall never see, and, those things I shall never do, *and it doesn't matter,* and I think of missed opportunities, what has been called the 'sin of an unlived life', which does matter.[74]

Mayne finishes the book on the strong note of gratitude. 'The dance' is a life-long lesson in learning to be grateful for all that is good and in knowing God's deep and abiding compassion in the midst of life's oftentimes harsh realities. Throughout the dance of life God offers us a love and acceptance which surpasses our understanding. Mayne writes in conclusion, "*Gratitude* and *grace*, I'll buy that for an epitaph. Or rather, I'll go on working at it, trusting that one day I may be confident enough to cast away my inhibitions and really learn to dance."[75]

NOTES

1. Michael Mayne, Letter to Brendan Walsh, 21 January 2000.
2. Michael Mayne, Letter to Brendan Walsh, 8 January 2001.
3. John Austin Baker, review of *Learning to Dance,* by Michael Mayne, *The Salisbury Cathedral News,* n. d.
4. Ibid.
5. Ibid.
6. Ibid.
7. Ibid.
8. Victor Stock, "Finding Your Still Centre," *Church Times*, 1 November 2002, 18.
9. Ibid.
10. David Scott, review of *Learning to Dance,* by Michael Mayne, *The Franciscan* 15 (May 2003): 14.
11. Margaret Silf, "Rhythm of Life," *The Tablet,* 18 May 2002, 25.
12. Ibid.
13. Ibid.
14. Ibid.
15. Ibid.
16. Ibid.
17. Ibid.
18. Review of *Learning to Dance,* by Michael Mayne, *Scientific and Medical Network Review,* n. d.
19. Ibid.
20. Mike Starkey, "Fireside Chat," *Christian Herald,* 9 February 2002, 7.
21. Ibid.
22. Rick Mercer, "Time With a Well-Stocked Mind," *Church Times,* 22 March 2002, 17.
23. Ibid., 14.
24. Ibid., 17.
25. Margaret McAllister, "What I'm Reading," *Church Times*, 28 September 2007, 22.
26. Ibid.
27. Review of *Learning to Dance,* by Michael Mayne, *Parish News,* February 2002, 6.

28. Patricia Billsborrow, "Travelling Down Spiritual and Theological Paths," *Methodist Recorder,* 31 January 2002.

29. Michael Mayne, *Learning to Dance* (London: Darton, Longman and Todd, 2001), ix.

30. Ibid.

31. Ibid., x.

32. Ibid.

33. Ibid., xi.

34. Ibid., 17.

35. Ibid., 189.

36. Ibid.

37. Ibid., 202.

38. Annie Dillard, *For the Time Being* (New York: Vintage Books, 1999), 144.

39. Richard Foster, "Introduction," in *The Sacrament of the Present Moment*, by Jean-Pierre De Caussade (New York: HarperSanFrancisco, 1981), xix.

40. Rick Mathis, *Finding a Grace-Filled Life* (New York: Paulist Press, 2008), 17.

41. Joan Chittister, *The Gift of Years: Growing Older Gracefully* (New York: BlueBridge, 2008), 169.

42. Mayne, *Learning to Dance*, 6.

43. Ibid., 7.

44. Ibid., 25.

45. Ibid., 26.

46. Ibid., 29.

47. Ibid., 95.

48. Rowan Williams, *Tokens of Trust: An Introduction to Christian Beliefs,* 37.

49. Ibid.

50. Dillard, *For the Time Being*, 72.

51. Michael Mayne, *Learning to Dance*, 35.

52. Rowan Williams, *Anglican Identities*, 43.

53. Hugh Montefiore, *Credible Christianity: The Gospel in Contemporary Society* (Grand Rapids: William B. Eerdmans Publishing Company, 1993), 277.

54. George Carey, *Why I Believe in a Personal God: The Credibility of Faith in a Doubting Culture* (Wheaton, IL: Harold Shaw Publishers, 1989), 137.

55. Mark Oakley, *The Collage of God*, 54.

56. John A. T. Robinson, *Honest to God* (Philadelphia: Westminster Press, 1963), 27.

57. George Carey, "Michael Ramsey's Response to *Honest To God,"* in *Michael Ramsey as Theologian,* ed. Robin Gill and Lorna Kendall (Cambridge, MA: Cowley Publications, 1995), 171.

58. Basil Hume, *The Mystery of the Incarnation* (London: Darton, Longman and Todd, 1999), 21.

59. Eric James, *A Life of Bishop John A. T. Robinson: Scholar, Pastor, Prophet,* 113.

60. George Connor, *Hints and Guesses II: Selected Commentaries, 1982 – 1997,* 124.

61. Oakley, 47.

62. Mayne, *Learning to Dance*, 3.

63. Ibid., 197.

64. Henri Nouwen, *Beloved: Henri Nouwen in Conversation* (Grand Rapids: William B. Eerdmans Publishing Company, 2007), 5.

65. George Connor, *Living With the Word* (Chattanooga: The George Connor Society, 2004), 71.

66. Annie Dillard, *Teaching a Stone to Talk: Expeditions and Encounters* (New York: HarperPerennial, 1982), 139.

67. Mayne, *Learning to Dance*, 166.

68. Ibid., 167.

69. Ibid.

70. Ibid., 168.

71. Ibid., 169.

72. Chittister, 123.

73. Mayne, *Learning to Dance,* 238.

74. Ibid., 229.

75. Ibid., 241.

CHAPTER FIVE

THE ENDURING MELODY

Approached by Darton, Longman and Todd for another book, Michael Mayne stood firm initially. *Learning to Dance* had, without question, been envisioned as the final book. In time, however, circumstances led Mayne to embrace the challenge of another writing project. He was considering a book which would address spirituality from the point of view of one nearing the end of life. This proposed piece would assess those spiritual ideas and commitments which endure to the end and which prove to be essential to a life of faith, as opposed to those components of the spiritual life which, in the end, are allowed to fall away, having proven to be nonessential. In the summer of 2005, Mayne was diagnosed with cancer of the jaw. He committed to write *The Enduring Melody* as an attempt to offer spiritual comfort and encouragement to others struggling in 'cancer country.' Parts I and II of the book are addresses Mayne had given before the diagnosis. They reflect his original idea regarding a final book, whose tentative target time of release was 2009. Part III is an astonishingly candid account of Mayne's experiences following the diagnosis. In the beginning there was hope that the cancer could be treated with some effectiveness, but after a long series of painful treatments the cancer proved terminal.

Peter Eaton describes this truly unique book as, "Part journal, part autobiography, part meditation, part theology, part prayer...."[1] Mayne himself refers to it as "rather mongrellish."[2] *The Enduring Melody* is an extraordinarily intimate autobiographical account of one person's passage from life to death. It is a haunting book, unforgettable in the deepest possible sense of that word. Within the first year of its publication the book had sold over 6,000 copies.

Brendan Walsh, Mayne's editor, received a letter dated 1 April 2006 from Michael Mayne announcing that the manuscript was nearing completion. Mayne was, at that time, suffering from severe dental pain from both the cancer and the treatments. He wrote, "I'm a shade low at present, and I'm determined to end the book on a high: an honest high which doesn't pretend that everything is rosy, but which says: 'I've come through, and life is good again.'"[3] At this point the diagnosis was not yet terminal. On 23 April 2006, Mayne wrote to Walsh about *The Enduring Melody,* "I'm hypercritical, and I'm pleased with it...."[4] He added, "I think, of all my books, it's the one I'd want to save in a fire...."[5] Suggesting a blurb for the book, Mayne wrote to Walsh:

> In this highly personal book Michael Mayne set out to tackle the linked questions of what is the solid ground of a belief which for him has proved authentic and survived into old age, and how aging may affect us physically, mentally and spiritually. That done, there came the unexpected challenge of cancer of the jaw, and in a nine-month journal he reflects (among much else) on whether his faith stands firm, and where God may be found in the challenging country of cancer.[6]

Writing to Mayne on 19 May 2006, Walsh said, "I think you've done a quite fabulous job. It feels absolutely real, and I'm sure this is why so many people love your books and have found something in them they have found in few other writers."[7]

The book is dedicated to four friends of Mayne's who died of cancer – Stewart Cross, who had been Bishop of Blackburn and a colleague of Mayne's at the BBC; John A. T. Robinson; Giles Eccleston, a successor of Mayne's at Great St. Mary's, Cambridge; and Terrence Wenham, a friend from Harpenden.

* * *

Thomas Moore, in *Dark Nights of the Soul: A Guide to Finding Your Way Through Life's Ordeals,* quotes Virginia Woolf from a piece titled "On Being Ill." Woolf writes:

> Considering how common illness is, how tremendous the spiritual change that it brings, how astonishing, when the lights of health go down, the undiscovered centuries that are then disclosed, what wastes and deserts of the soul a slight attack of influenza brings to view, what precipices and lawns sprinkled with bright flowers a little rise of temperature reveals, what ancient and obdurate oaks are uprooted in us by the act of sickness. . . it is strange indeed that illness has not taken its place with love and battle and jealousy among the prime themes of literature.[8]

Along these lines, David M. Hoyle, in the Mere's Sermon at Corpus Christi College, Cambridge, published in 2007, describes *The Enduring Melody* as a "searingly honest account of what it is to think about dying."[9] Eamon Duffy, in his memorial sermon for Mayne at Great St. Mary's, Cambridge, refers to the book as "a harrowing chronicle of hope and endurance in the face of indignity and very great suffering. It is impossible to read it without tears, and it is his best book."[10] *The Daily Telegraph's* obituary for Mayne notes that the book was written "to help his fellow sufferers."[11] Donald Gray, in his obituary for Mayne in *Church Times*, writes that the book recounts "a heroic end that will inspire many."[12]

The back cover of Richard John Neuhaus' *As I Lay Dying: Meditations Upon Returning*, describes that book as "sometimes grim but always graceful...." Though unquestionably difficult to read at times, there is also a gracefulness, a dignity which suffuses *The Enduring Melody*.

In the obituary for Mayne in *The Tablet*, Anthony Harvey writes that, "The book...reveals the integration of faith, pastoral experience and aesthetic sensibility which had been at work in his life from the time when, as a small boy, he had to face the suicide of his father...."[13] In the obituary in *The Independent on Sunday* Harvey describes *The Enduring Melody* as, "An astonishingly frank and compelling account...."[14] He considers the book to be "a remarkable testimony" which has been "received and treasured by many."[15] In Mayne's obituary posted on the Westminster Abbey website, Robert Wright notes that the book "will be of enormous help to both those who face their own death and those who support the dying."[16]

Writing in *The Pastoral Review*, Anne Long states, "If you want to be inspired by an account of someone living out every moment of his dying then you are likely to be moved and challenged at a deep and lasting level."[17] She observes that the book contains "gems of reflection on literature, words, art, relationships...wonder, God, the Church, incarnation, prayer, death."[18] She advises, "Read it and re-read it for in it you will find treasures you will want to return to again and again."[19]

In her review for *The Times*, Salley Vickers writes:

> What is so remarkable about *The Enduring Melody* is its unsentimental testimony to the power of faith and hope not to banish but to grow alongside pain and loss as a realisable potential of consciousness. It is a brave and moving account of one man's effort to celebrate life at its most testing and inexplicable, and as such will bring a sense of comprehending companionship to others undergoing similar trials.[20]

Barrie Hibbert, in a sermon preached at Flinders Street Baptist Church in Adelaide, Australia, says of the book, "It is not easy to read...in fact it gets harder as you go...but as you go, you become more and more aware that you are walking on holy ground."[21] Hibbert observes that Mayne "was writing his own obituary."[22] In a sermon preached on Good Friday, 2007, at St. Dunstan-in-the-West parish in London, William Gulliford states regarding *The Enduring Melody*, "It is a staggering book, which I had to read in stages not because it is dense, but because it is so vivid."[23]

Writing in *Church Times*, Sr. Frances Dominica notes, "When I started to read this book, I found myself putting markers in pages to which I wanted to return – and then I stopped, because I was marking every other page. The book is a treasury."[24] Writing in *The Tablet*, James Roose-Evans states, "The harvest of a lifetime has been gathered in these pages and it invites several readings."[25] He suggests that the book is in the tradition of George Herbert.[26] Joyce Donoghue, reviewing the book in the newsletter of Holy Trinity Church,

Cuckfield (Sussex) writes, "This is a story of pain and death faced with great courage and, despite the ending, not a sad book but rather an encouragement to those of us with a lesser faith and, so far, less pain to bear."[27]

In a review for *The Observer* dated 17 September 2006, Robert McCrum writes:

> At the moment...Michael Mayne is terminally ill, but with the publication of this courageous book, he will have in his final weeks the consolation of knowing that, in this unflinching, brave and unforgettable memoir, he has provided a dispatch from the front line of ill health that will provide comfort for thousands in the future.[28]

In McCrum's view, "There will be few more affecting books this autumn."[29] Writing in *OKS Offcuts,* Roger Symon states that Mayne has left behind "an inspirational classic of Christian spirituality."[30]

* * *

Though Mayne lived to see the publication of the book, most of the letters to him from appreciative readers arrived after his death. One reader writes, "Your new book is masterly – a classic description of the advent of death. It deserves to be a resounding success, not a short term sensation but a quiet influence on many people for years to come." Another letter notes that Mayne's selections of quotations and thoughts from others are "more than matched" by his own prose. A reader writes, "As an example of how to deal with adversity it is unparalleled in my experience." Another writes, "I shall keep returning to it. . . ."

A bishop in the Church of England notes, "Your writing is deep, searching – and liberating when fully 'taken on board.'" He adds, "It ought to be required reading in theological colleges and in clergy study groups." He concludes, "I thank you for your book, which is so searching, so challenging – and (I must say) so deeply moving." Another reader suggests, "It should certainly be compulsory reading for all doctors!" In a letter dated 26 October 2006, four days after Mayne's death, a reader writes that the book is "profoundly moving." The person goes on to say poignantly, "Your willingness to share the painful journey through 'the questioning country of cancer' with such honesty and humour is infinitely helpful to those, like myself, whose own journey is just beginning."

In a letter to Mayne's publisher, a reader, having just experienced the sudden, unexpected death of someone very dear to them, writes on 18 October 2006, "I find it to be the very greatest help, the very greatest help, and of such intelligence, insight and understanding which perhaps can only come through very great suffering." This person adds, "I have received all he says into my very broken heart." Another reader writes to Mayne that *The Enduring Melody* is "without doubt the most moving book I have read."

As people heard the news of her husband's death, Alison Mayne began receiving letters regarding *The Enduring Melody*. One states, "I've given *The Enduring Melody* to six people all of whom have welcomed it gratefully and join me in blessing your husband for having written it." Another reader writes, "I read [from] it nearly every day." Another observes, "It is so packed with wisdom and reflection that it is hard to be read at a stretch...."

In a letter to Alison Mayne, Mark Mayne, and Sarah Mayne Tyndall dated 23 October 2006 Brendan Walsh writes, "Michael was an inspiration to me and I was so proud to have worked with him: his books will rattle around the world for as long as people will wonder about love and justice and prayer and forgiveness."

* * *

In typical modesty, Michael Mayne writes in the introduction to *The Enduring Melody* that he had been "confident" that four books were "more than enough," and that everything he had to say had been said by the end of *Learning to Dance*.[31] Anyone who reads his final book, however, realizes that *The Enduring Melody* stands out – everything that comes before it in his body of work leads up to, but does not fully anticipate, the contents of his last literary work. He states in the introduction that the book is his honest attempt to write about his time in 'the questioning country of cancer', a term he learned from Mother Mary John of the Benedictine community at West Malling.[32] He makes clear that the final text of the book is printed largely as it was originally written.[33] Echoing his earlier thoughts regarding *A Year Lost and Found*, this final book is offered to encourage others in their experience of darkness. Mayne writes, "I believe that one of the ways in which God can use our experience of darkness is to increase our imaginative understanding, reaching out to one another with love because we have been there too."[34]

Mayne defines *cantus firmus* from the language of music as the firm ground, the absolute rather than that which is relative. The *cantus firmus*, the enduring melody, is that which endures throughout, as opposed to that which proves nonessential.[35] He affirms that the *cantus firmus* is unique for each individual, as each human being experiences life from an absolutely unique perspective.[36] Through to his final work, Mayne is consistent in his theme of the (ultimately) "unbridgeable aloneness" of every individual.[37] Mayne assures his readers that in God's love and mercy one can stand before God without pretense or fear, for:

This uniqueness that is 'me' is what I have to offer my Creator, who knows me infinitely better than I know myself, and graciously welcomes me home, not in spite of what I have been but because of what I am. 'Graciously': the action of grace. 'Home': the place where I can shed all pretence, where 'everything is known and yet forgiven'.[38]

Later in the book he notes that biographers must admit that they cannot possibly penetrate through a person's protective layers to know "the full secrets of any human heart."[39]

In *Pray, Love, Remember* Mayne writes regarding the finality of death that when that time comes, "We cannot hold on to anything...."[40] And in *Learning to Dance* he admits that prior to our death, no individual can know for sure what their response will be.[41] Though not yet diagnosed as terminal, with the cancer known Mayne acknowledges in *The Enduring Melody* that all he has written, preached, and counseled will now be put to the test.[42] While anticipating the unknown of an upcoming operation Mayne writes in his diary on 13 July 2005, "'Your right hand holds me fast' battles with moments of panic."[43] The entry of 14 July admits that like any other person, he experiences moments of strength, and then moments of fear.[44]

The entry for 19 July admits that, his best efforts to the contrary notwithstanding, he still falls prey to the temptation to take things for granted.[45] The current illness reminds Mayne powerfully of his many blessings.

In the entry for 28 July, he acknowledges his first real sense of "desolation."[46] While recovering from extensive and painful surgery, he writes on 10 August about the "dark days" of the difficult period of recovery, but that, in retrospect, he recognizes God's presence.[47]

The entry for 18 August mentions the tragic murder of Brother Roger of the Taizé community. Mayne had known Brother Roger and, along with Christians worldwide, is devastated by the news of Brother Roger's violent death at the hand of a mentally disturbed person. Most interestingly, Mayne states that of all the people he has met in his life and through his very visible postings five stand out as the most exceptional – Nelson Mandela, Mother Teresa, the Dalai Lama, Desmond Tutu, and "by no means least," Brother Roger.[48]

Mayne's approach to his battle with cancer was influenced in no small measure by his friend John A. T. Robinson's own experience in the early 1980s. On 24 August 2005 Mayne writes that he finds God "in" the evil of the cancer. Importantly, Mayne notes that he does not believe that God sent the cancer, but that God "is to be found in and through it...."[49] Mayne knew well and had great respect for Robinson's courageous and dignified battle with the illness. In a sermon at Trinity College Chapel, Cambridge, Robinson stated, "For God is to be found in the cancer as in everything else. If he is not, then he is not the God of the Psalmist who said, 'If I go down to hell, thou art there also', let alone of the Christian who knows God most deeply in the Cross."[50] On 11 September 2005 Mayne writes that though not necessarily a death sentence, cancer is an unrelenting "tap on the shoulder" regarding one's mortality. Unlike a sudden, unexpected death, or the slow, gradual decline into senility, cancer [typically] allows one time to "say what needs to be said."[51] On 9 July 1983, Robinson wrote in his journal that a diagnosis of cancer [typically] allows one to "prepare and make dispositions with the family...."[52] On 8 June 1983 Robinson had written, "I always used to think the words in Bishop Ken's hymn: 'Live this day as 'twere' thy last' rather morbid, but I now know what they mean: to count and enjoy every moment that is given you...."[53]

Mayne's entry for 22 – 23 September 2005 reckons honestly and hauntingly with the prospect of the fear of death. He writes that "there's a sense in which we are human before we are Christian and the very human bit retains that primal fear of the dark, the unknown...."[54]

As Mayne's illness progressed, his journal entries became less frequent and more general. The entry for May 2006 recalls a major point of *A Year Lost and Found* that a patient longs to be treated as a whole person and not merely as a set of symptoms. He writes:

> Each of us is frail and vulnerable; too often we are to be discovered sitting in the doctor's waiting room, or lying in a hospital bed or on a psychiatrist's couch, crying out for healing. Crying out to be seen, not chiefly as a set of interesting symptoms or a machine requiring repair, but as a person, with all that word implies.[55]

In the postscript of *The Enduring Melody* Mayne writes with absolute, unflinching honesty about learning that the long, extensive, and very painful treatments in the end have not worked and that the cancer has returned with full force. These pages are a window into this man's soul, insofar as such is possible. He writes of his desire to die with gratitude for all of the blessings of his life and without resentment for the illness that is taking his life.

Gillian Rose's extraordinary book, *Love's Work: A Reckoning with Life*, contains the haunting passage, "I went through this [cancer treatment] for the whole summer, every ten days; all, it transpired, to no avail. My well-differentiated cancer is chemotherapy-resistant."[56] An engaged reader is moved to the core by such finality, for as Mayne would put it, we are first of all human, and, at the deepest core of our being, we cannot help but be frightened of the ultimate unknown. Michael Mayne's final written words acknowledge both his unspeakable sadness and his ultimate hopefulness in the faith that endures.

NOTES

1. Peter Eaton, "A Rich Life: The Writings of Michael Mayne," 19.
2. Michael Mayne, *The Enduring Melody* (London: Darton, Longman and Todd, 2006), xviii.
3. Michael Mayne, Letter to Brendan Walsh, 1 April 2006.
4. Michael Mayne, Letter to Brendan Walsh, 23 April 2006.
5. Ibid.
6. Ibid.
7. Brendan Walsh, Letter to Michael Mayne, 19 May 2006.
8. Thomas Moore, *Dark Nights of the Soul: A Guide to Finding Your Way Through Life's Ordeals* (New York: Gotham Books, 2004), 268.

9. David M. Hoyle, "Mere's Sermon," *Letter of the Corpus Association*, Corpus Christi College, Cambridge, Michaelmas 2007, 27.

10. Eamon Duffy, sermon preached at Great St. Mary's (The University Church), Cambridge, for a Eucharist of Remembering and Thanksgiving for Michael Mayne, 6.

11. Obituary for Michael Mayne, *The Daily Telegraph*, 24 October 2006, 27.

12. Donald Gray, Obituary for Michael Mayne, *Church Times,* 27.

13. Anthony Harvey, Obituary for Michael Mayne, *The Tablet*, 40.

14. Anthony Harvey, Obituary for Michael Mayne, *The Independent on Sunday,* 28 October 2006, 3.

15. Anthony Harvey, Personal correspondence, 19 October 2008.

16. Obituary for Michael Mayne, Westminster Abbey, 1.

17. Anne Long, review of *The Enduring Melody*, by Michael Mayne, *The Pastoral Review* 4 (May/June 2008): 94.

18. Ibid.

19. Ibid.

20. Salley Vickers, review of *The Enduring Melody*, by Michael Mayne, *The Times,* 29 July 2006.

21. Barrie Hibbert, "The Bottom Line," sermon preached at Flinders Street Baptist Church, Adelaide, Australia, 26 November 2006, 3.

22. Ibid., 2.

23. William Gulliford, "Good Friday Sermon 2007," sermon preached at St. Dunstan-in-the-West, London, 6 April 2007, 1.

24. Dominica, Sister Frances, "Singer at One with His Song," *Church Times*, 30 March 2007, 25.

25. James Roose-Evans, "Heroic Last Testament," *The Tablet*, 4 November 2006, 24.

26. Ibid.

27. Joyce Donoghue, review of *The Enduring Melody,* by Michael Mayne, *Making Christ Known: Holy Trinity, Cuckfield Parish Magazine,* April 2007, 17.

28. Robert McCrum, "Hope Lives on in Cancer Country," *The Observer.*

29. Ibid.

30. Roger Symon, review of *The Enduring Melody*, by Michael Mayne, *OKS Offcuts,* 19 January 2007, 7.

31. Michael Mayne, *The Enduring Melody*, xv.

32. Ibid., xvii.

33. Ibid.

34. Ibid., xx.

35. Ibid., 3.

36. Ibid., 8.

37. Ibid., 21.

38. Ibid., 33.

39. Ibid., 101.

40. Michael Mayne, *Pray, Love, Remember*, 117.

41. Michael Mayne, *Learning to Dance*, 158.

42. Mayne, *The Enduring Melody*, 48.

43. Ibid., 49.

44. Ibid., 51.

45. Ibid., 55.

46. Ibid., 70.

47. Ibid., 80.

48. Ibid., 93.

49. Ibid., 123.

50. Eric James, *A Life of Bishop John A. T. Robinson: Scholar, Pastor, Prophet, 291.*

51. Mayne, *The Enduring Melody*, 169.

52. James, 291.

53. Ibid., 286.

54. Michael Mayne, *The Enduring Melody*, 190.

55. Ibid., 242.

56. Gillian Rose, *Love's Work: A Reckoning With Life* (New York: Schocken Books, 1995), 89.

CONCLUSION

At the time of the death of Michael Ramsey, George Connor wrote a column for the newsletter of St. Peter's Episcopal Church in Chattanooga, Tennessee. The column is a tribute to the former archbishop and reads in part, "Ramsey was a deeply spiritual man and Anglican to the bone. We all have cause to thank God for his life and work; may he rest in peace."[1] Connor could just as well have been describing his friend, Michael Mayne. Mayne, like Ramsey, was Anglican to the bone. When one thinks of a well-educated, urbane English cleric, Michael Mayne fits that description. Mayne served the Church of England his entire adult life. A faithful parish priest, diocesan staff member, and broadcasting executive, in time he rose to serve in one of the most visible pastoral posts in the Christian church. A pastor first, he was also a writer whose books have sold more than 38,000 copies and remain in print. In his study are hundreds of letters from readers who, in the end, say essentially the same thing – thank you.

Mayne penned the introduction to the 1998 reprint of Anthony Trollope's *Clergymen of the Church of England*. There he writes that the defining marks of Anglicanism are:

> Tolerance within a broad spectrum of belief and interpretation, a high regard for the individual conscience; moderation in face of extremism; a recognition that sometimes the truth lies in both extremes rather than somewhere in between.[2]

Mayne's own ministry and his writings were guided by these principles. In the same piece he writes that while in the Anglican tradition the cleric is priest and preacher, the cleric is chiefly pastor, whose work is classically defined in the life and writings of George Herbert, the chief component of the work being "the care and cure of souls."[3]

In his book, *The Gift of Peace*, Joseph Cardinal Bernadin writes:

> People look to priests to be authentic witnesses to God's active role in the world, to his love. They don't want us to be politicians or business managers; they are not interested in the petty conflicts that may show up in parish or diocesan life. Instead, people simply want us to be with them in the joys and sorrows of their lives.[4]

In person, and through his writings, Mayne was with people in both their joys and their sorrows. John Waller, who knew Mayne in Harpenden, and then later in retirement in Salisbury, suggests that Mayne's three "demanding" appointments (the BBC, Cambridge, and Westminster) allowed him "to move among people on the margins of the Church, and outside it."[5] In Waller's view, "This fed him as he fed them"[6] Waller states further, "In Michael I saw someone living out the thoughts he expressed in his books."[7] He adds, "I experienced Michael as a pilgrim on the move."[8]

In her book *Leaving Church: A Memoir of Faith,* Barbara Brown Taylor observes, "Being ordained is not about serving God perfectly but about serving God visibly, allowing people to learn whatever they can from watching you rise and fall."[9] Mayne served God visibly through his writings as well as his various ministries. With a proper reticence so important to him, he allowed himself to be vulnerable as an encouragement to others in their own struggles. This book is not an exercise in hagiography. It is about a priest who was honest.

Near the end of his ministry at Westminster, Mayne published a small booklet titled *Something Understood: Talks on Prayer.* This is not one of his major books as far as visibility or number of sales, but it is nonetheless an excellent piece that deserves attention. In it he writes:

> Those who write books, or preach sermons, or give addresses on prayer, do so because of what they *lack*, not because of what they *have*. I have spoken of what I *long for*, not of what I possess; of how I would *like* to be, not of what I am. Of one who travels with you on the journey, sometimes tentatively, often not very confidently, yet always with hope,'looking to Jesus, the author and perfecter of our faith.'[10]

Annie Dillard claims in *The Writing Life,* "The impulse to keep to yourself what you have learned is not only shameful, it is destructive. Anything you do not give freely and abundantly becomes lost to you."[11] In many ways Mayne was a reluctant writer. *A Year Lost and Found* was envisioned as a 'small' book. Its author never dreamed that it would be a bestseller and elicit appreciative letters from all over the world. *This Sunrise of Wonder* was his 'big book.' *Pray, Love, Remember* was his 'love letter' to Westminster in thanksgiving for ten fruitful and fulfilling years at the abbey. *Learning to Dance* was an unanticipated kind of sequel to *This Sunrise of Wonder. The Enduring Melody,* in the end, proved to be a project that Mayne obviously did not envision in the way that circumstances eventually dictated. In *The Enduring Melody* the author states that however mixed a writer's motives may be, in the end [good] writing is about the desire to speak helpfully to the human condition. He notes, "For those who write such books, and nervously launch them into a critical world, they aim to be, in short, a small – and sometimes quite risky – act of love."[12] Salley Vickers says of Mayne that he is "never pompous or pious," yet at the same time "a deep vein of piety runs discreetly beneath everything he says...."[13]

    In a funeral sermon preached at Salisbury Cathedral on 3 November 2006, Jeremy Davies says:

> However humbly, he [Mayne] walked the corridors of power, he wore the scarlet of the Queen's Household and met, and in many cases knew well, the movers and shakers of our world. But he was never seduced by grandeur or confined by the Church of England, love it though he did.[14]

    In his slim book, *Jesus and Mary: Finding Our Sacred Center,* Henri Nouwen quotes Mother Teresa, who once told him, "Write simply...very simply. People need simple words."[15] Though erudite, Mayne's books are, at the same time, unfailingly accessible. In his memoir, *The Road to Daybreak: A Spiritual Journey,* Nouwen recalls a friend saying to him, "I hope you find time to write, but don't take yourself too seriously!"[16] Mayne's modesty, and his sense of humor are evident in his writings. In the tapes of his addresses at the Bowen conference, they are on display in abundance.

    In *The Yellow Leaves: A Miscellany,* Frederick Buechner states, "I went on my own way as a writer, alternately depressed or elated by the reviewers but never seriously influenced by them."[17] Mayne found his own writing style and was true to himself, to his unique perspective. He makes absolutely no claim to being an original thinker. In a review of Morton T. Kelsey's *Caring: How Can We Love One Another?,* George Connor writes, "There is perhaps little in the book that a reader is likely to find wholly new, but as Samuel Johnson once said, we need to be reminded more often than we need to be taught."[18] In the preface to his *Credo,* William Sloane Coffin writes, "Now that my years appear to be hastening to their end, I want to acknowledge how much I owe to my many, many teachers. Believe me, a totally original idea is a remarkable rarity."[19] Richard H. Schmidt, in *Glorious Companions: Five Centuries of Anglican Spirituality,* recalls C. S. Lewis saying of one of his books that if anything in it was original it was "so against my will and as a result of my ignorance."[20] To have not been an original theological thinker in no way mitigates the keenness of Mayne's intellect. The obituary for Mayne in the *Letter of the Corpus Association* reflects in part on his tenure at Great St. Mary's, Cambridge, where, "He is remembered for his outstanding preaching and pastoral gifts and his ability to keep up with his colleagues in academic theology."[21]

    Regarding Mayne's way with words, spoken or written, Nicholas Sagovsky, in his sermon for Mayne's memorial service at Westminster, states, "There was no finer craftsman than Michael."[22] Sagovsky adds, "He was himself a consummate communicator – some would say the best preacher they ever heard."[23] According to Sagovsky:

> No other spiritual writer has a voice quite like his: diarist, essayist, mystic, wit – what he wrote was utterly English, with echoes of Donne and Traherne, Kilvert and Blythe – the range is extraordinary. His books draw us in because, like a trusted friend, he confides in his reader; no wonder so many readers confided in him.[24]

In the opinion of Rowan Williams, "The importance of what he [Mayne] writes is primarily...in its candour about the growth that happens through vulnerability...."[25] Frederick Buechner would agree, as he finds Mayne's work "full of human truth and unfailing honesty."[26] In his work *The Book of Buechner: A Journey Through His Writings*, W. Dale Brown, echoing Buechner's own understanding, notes, "We all of us walk with a limp."[27] Mayne was not afraid to acknowledge his.

Elizabeth Vardaman says of Mayne: "I know of no one who was speaking so powerfully through the arts, in concert with scripture, to the life of the spirit and the radiance of God's revelation through nature, music, theatre, and most poignantly, the work of great poets."[28] With particular reference to *The Enduring Melody*, Ronald Blythe observes that Mayne, "Was able to give a language to suffering which complemented that of medicine. In this he was a genius."[29]

In Peter Eaton's opinion, Mayne has left us, "Not one classic of the literature of spirituality in the Anglican tradition, but five...."[30] Samuel H. Dresner, editor of Abraham Joshua Heschel's *I Asked for Wonder: A Spiritual Anthology*, writes that Heschel, like his hasidic forbears had the gift of combining "profundity with simplicity."[31] Such is the case with Mayne. Philip Yancey writes of G. K. Chesterton and C. S. Lewis that they "combined sophisticated taste with a humility that did not demean others."[32] Likewise, Mayne wrote his books with a pastor's sensitivity and touch.

More often than not, Mayne was inclined to quote writers other than theologians, for, "I have learned much more about human nature – and, I believe, about the transcendent, about good and evil, sin and grace – from the novelist and poet than from the theologian."[33] Here one is reminded of Anna Quindlen's claim, "I'm a novelist. My work is human nature. *Real life* (emphasis mine) is really all I know."[34]

From real life Michael Mayne knew about the loss of his father from suicide. Nicholas Sagovsky notes that this "unmistakable note of loss" was written indelibly in the *cantus firmus* of Mayne's life.[35] He observes, "Somehow or other that deficit was turned into an extraordinary sympathy with those on the margin."[36]

* * *

Those who knew Mayne refer to a streak of perfectionism in him. In *Learning to Dance*, he himself acknowledges how much time he has "wasted" in a kind of "anxious perfectionism."[37] Eamon Duffy notes regarding the death of Mayne's father from suicide, "All that flowed from it had left in this man, so talented, so blessed in his marriage, so poised and apparently so at home with the great and the good, a core of vulnerability and anxious unease which drove him to perfectionism."[38] This core of vulnerability Mayne himself acknowledged, and it led him to his unusual capacity for compassion. In *No*

Future Without Forgiveness Desmond Tutu cautions, "We should be generous in our judgment of others, for we can never really know all there is to know about another."[39] Similarly, Joan Chittister notes, "Is there anyone we wouldn't love, poet Mary Lou Kownacki writes, if we only knew their story?"[40] Barbara Brown Taylor reminds us that it was Philo of Alexandria who said, "Be kind...for everyone you meet is fighting a great battle."[41]

* * *

One of the great strengths of Mayne's work is his acceptance of the unanswerable mysteries regarding the nature of the divine. He would agree completely with Peter Gomes, who writes in *The Good Book: Reading the Bible with Mind and Heart,* "Religion is not the answer to the unknowable or the unfaceable or the unendurable; religion is what we do and what we are in the face of the unknowable, the unfaceable, and the unendurable."[42] As Mark Oakley puts it, "Faith is not a proud self-consistent philosophy. It involves maintaining oneself between contradictions that can't be solved by analysis."[43] William Sloane Coffin cautions, "The worst thing we can do with a dilemma is to resolve it prematurely because we haven't the courage to live with the uncertainty."[44] Coffin acknowledges that there are those who "prefer certainty to truth...."[45] He then adds, "And what a distortion of the gospel it is to have limited sympathies and unlimited certainties, when the very reverse – to have limited certainties and unlimited sympathies – is not only more tolerant but far more Christian."[46] He continues, "Seekers of truth can build communities of love. Possessors of truth have too much enmity toward those who don't possess the truth, or possess some other truth."[47]

* * *

It is rare to find a writer who can counsel a life of joy and gratitude while at the same time readily acknowledging the harsh, oftentimes cruel realities of life. Michael Mayne does this as well and as consistently as any modern author. He would agree with Barbara Brown Taylor that, "True bliss is never more than a hair away from sorrow."[48]

* * *

In *Finding a Grace-Filled Life,* Rick Mathis notes that "reading...is an intensely personal experience...."[49] What constitutes good literature is a subjective judgment based on one's tastes, one's temperament, and one's life experiences. Michael Mayne is not the best selling spiritual writer of our time. Nor will he be. There are those who find his work unoriginal, and thus, in the end, unexceptional. But there are those who judge him to be one of the very finest of all those who write regarding matters of faith. For some, he is their favorite modern author, speaking to their uniqueness, to their particular situation, to their own human condition more compellingly than any other spiritual writer.

Mayne writes in *Learning to Dance*: "And it is that dance of words that have been my lifelong delight...."[50] His writings are a testament to his passion for and breadth of learning, and to his own very considerable giftedness in 'the dance.' Michael Mayne's words will stand the test of time and will take their place among the very finest of Anglican pastoral writings. Through his writings, his ministry will endure.

NOTES

1. George Connor, *Hints and Guesses II: Selected Commentaries, 1982 – 1997*, 73.
2. Michael Mayne, "Introduction," in *Clergymen of the Church of England,* by Anthony Trollope (London: The Trollope Society, 1998), xii.
3. Ibid., xi.
4. Joseph Cardinal Bernadin, *The Gift of Peace* (London: Darton, Longman and Todd, 1998), 89.
5. John Waller, Personal correspondence.
6. Ibid.
7. Ibid.
8. Ibid.
9. Barbara Brown Taylor, *Leaving Church: A Memoir of Faith*, 37.
10. Michael Mayne, *Something Understood: Talks on Prayer* (London: Barnard and Westwood, 1996), 23.
11. Annie Dillard, *The Writing Life,* 79.
12. Michael Mayne, *The Enduring Melody*, 245.
13. Salley Vickers, review of *The Enduring Melody,* by Michael Mayne.
14. Jeremy Davies, "Gratitude and Grace," sermon preached at Salisbury Cathedral for the Funeral Mass of Michael Mayne, 3 November 2006, 3.
15. Henri Nouwen, *Jesus & Mary: Finding Our Sacred Center* (Cincinnati: St. Anthony Messenger Press, 1993), 61.
16. Henri Nouwen, *The Road to Daybreak: A Spiritual Journey* (New York: Image Books, 1990), 146.
17. Frederick Buechner, *The Yellow Leaves: A Miscellany*, 46.
18. George Connor, *Living With the Word*, 53.
19. William Sloane Coffin, *Credo* (Louisville: Westminster John Knox Press, 2004), xvi.
20. Richard H. Schmidt, *Glorious Companions: Five Centuries of Anglican Spirituality* (Grand Rapids: William B. Eerdmans Publishing Company, 2003), 278.
21. Obituary for Michael Mayne, *Letter of the Corpus Association* (Cambridge: Corpus Christi College, 2007), 74.
22. Nicholas Sagovsky, sermon preached at Westminster Abbey for the Memorial Service for Michael Mayne, 1.
23. Ibid.
24. Ibid., 2.

25. Rowan Williams, Personal correspondence.

26. Frederick Buechner, Personal correspondence, 15 October 2008.

27. W. Dale Brown, *The Book of Buechner: A Journey Through His Writings* (Louisville: Westminster John Knox Press, 2006), 315.

28. Elizabeth Vardaman, Personal correspondence.

29. Ronald Blythe, "Word from Wormingford," *Church Times*, 3 November 2006, 40.

30. Peter Eaton, "A Rich Life: The Writings of Michael Mayne, " 19.

31. Samuel H. Dresner, in Abraham Joshua Heschel, *I Asked for Wonder: A Spiritual Anthology*, ed. Samuel H. Dresner (New York: The Crossroad Publishing Company, 1983), 13.

32. Philip Yancey, *Soul Survivor: How Thirteen Unlikely Mentors Helped My Faith Survive the Church,* 43.

33. Michael Mayne, *The Enduring Melody*, 170.

34. Anna Quindlen, *A Short Guide to a Happy Life* (New York: Random House, 2000), 4.

35. Nicholas Sagovsky, sermon preached at Westminster Abbey for the Memorial Service for Michael Mayne, 2.

36. Ibid.

37. Michael Mayne, *Learning to Dance*, 230.

38. Eamon Duffy, sermon preached at Great St. Mary's (The University Church), Cambridge, for a Eucharist of Remembering and Thanksgiving for Michael Mayne, 4.

39. Desmond Tutu, *No Future Without Forgiveness* (New York: Image Books, 1999), 169.

40. Joan Chittister, *The Gift of Years: Growing Older Gracefully,* 192.

41. Taylor, 230.

42. Peter Gomes, *The Good Book: Reading the Bible with Mind and Heart*, 213.

43. Mark Oakley, *The Collage of God*, xvii.

44. Coffin, 125.

45. Ibid., 144.

46. Ibid.

47. Ibid., 157.

48. Taylor, 97.

49. Rich Mathis, *Finding a Grace-Filled Life,* 82.

50. Mayne, *Learning to Dance*, 115.

AFTERWORD

It pleases me in the deep heart's core that Dr. Joel Huffstetler is introducing Michael Mayne's luminous texts to an American readership. One might have wished this conversation to have begun in the United States 20 years sooner, just after Dean Mayne's first book received a warm reception in the United Kingdom. Such blessings are thus long overdue in our country but, fortunately and joyfully, with this publication, the situation has been rectified. *Gratitude and Grace,* by explicating all of Michael's books and by referencing in the process so many important theological texts from our own tradition, provides a powerful and poignant overview of Michael Mayne's oeuvre and magnifies the need to have his books more readily available in the United States.

My good fortune in being introduced to Dean Mayne's writings early on occurred only because I was in the right place at the right time. My husband, James, was a professor of British history at Baylor University in Waco, Texas, and directed a summer study abroad program for many years in England. Incredibly, with support from our university, he had successfully negotiated with Westminster School in 1982 to house and board our students there. Thus for the next 20 summers, Baylor faculty and students claimed Victoria Tower, the Houses of Parliament, Big Ben, St. Margaret's Church, and Westminster Abbey as our neighborhood. We reveled in going out from and coming in to our "home" in Westminster School, tucked within the Abbey grounds (and many of us tried to look "English" as we did so).

Time seemed to wrinkle as we stepped across centuries of gravestones and traipsed the cloistered halls to breakfasts and dinners in what had long ago been the monks' refectory. Daily we had tea in an underground "dungeon" and heard the Westminster Choir Boys rehearsing, lifting their inspired voices (along with our thoughts) straight to celestial heights as we moved across Dean's Yard and Little Dean's Yard and into the bustling life of London and then happily back into the tranquil "bits at the back," of the Abbey environs.

In the midst of this splendor, my free time was often spent poking about in the array of book stores that filled the city centre; there, the smorgasbord of British and Irish novels, poetry, plays, and history seemed an embarrassment of riches. Each August as we packed to head home, my suitcases bulged with treasures such as Ronald Blythe's *Divine Landscapes*, a book of ruminations and historical walks across England through which Blythe pays his respects to Langland, Bunyan, Julian, and Herbert. (I re-read that book so many times I am certain I could have made those treks without a map!)

Based on my reputation for savoring books like Blythe's, one of my
English friends on staff at Westminster School suggested I might like "the new
dean's book that everyone was talking about." Purchasing *A Year Lost and
Found* at the Abbey Bookshop that day, I crossed Victoria Street, and headed to
St. James Park, where, under a spreading copper beech, I lay in the grass and
read a story that spoke straight to my soul—a direct transfusion of truth and
faith.

The clergyman's voice revealed the saga of a year at Great St. Mary's
Church in Cambridge wherein he and his family had searched for medical and
spiritual answers to heal a mysterious illness that had befallen him. I had never
read anything like it, even though John Claypool's *Tracks of a Fellow Struggler*
had introduced me to the sorrow and grief of a minister who had lost his beloved
daughter. This English priest touched my heart because he was so bewildered
by what had happened to him and at times seemed to pursue healing and understanding with an almost wild intensity. Yet no matter how much he wrestled
with the mystifying disease and searched for wholeness, he remained steadfast
in his affirmation of an incarnate world. Most importantly, the way this writer
presented his sojourn rang true to the human condition any of us might face.
Somehow he invested me, as reader, with privileges that let me become a companion on the road that he was traveling.

Thus, with the turning of each page, I identified more with Michael
Mayne's journey, despite having no pressing professional qualms, spiritual cri-
ses, or health challenges to confound me. I was just a seeker, trying always to
learn from authentic, erudite pilgrims who were leading the way to a deeper,
more insightful understanding of how to be God's people. It was clear as I finished the book that afternoon that Michael Mayne's questioning, searching and
travail had become, somehow, pillars upon which God was building this priest's
future. Since I knew the "rest of the story" that had transpired after the book was
completed (and is noted in the postscript), I walked "home" from the park with a
sense of exhilaration and epiphany:

> *This priest, now "my" priest, has been healed. He has even been chosen by
> God and Queen Elizabeth II to become Dean of Westminster Abbey! I can hear
> him next Sunday! Maybe I can ask him to sign my book!*

***

As I look back from the vantage point of years, that blowsy July afternoon in the park becomes a touchstone. Because of *A Year Lost and Found*, I
gained a heady sense that I could be included in a vital, fresh conversation about
illness, renewal and obedience to God's purposes.

Not long after reading Dean Mayne's book, my husband and I were
formally introduced to him and his wife, Alison. We had tea in their home a few
weeks later and talked about authors whose works meant the world to us. Then,
because life sometimes offers incredible serendipities, the next day they had a

hand-written invitation hand-delivered to our door, inviting us to have dinner with them and "a special guest" at the Deanery. Shortly after we arrived that evening, their dear friend, Ronald Blythe, walked in the door. My husband had taught Blythe's *Akenfield* in many British history classes, and I had, of course, walked across England with him. We ate together at the Maynes' pine table. The conversation was unlike any we had ever had before. We kept pinching ourselves – just to be sure we were not dreaming.

Then, as way led onto way, we settled into the reality that, incredibly, the friendship was real. Even though the Maynes were busy beyond comprehension, receiving heads of state and conducting national services within this "Royal Peculiar" Abbey, they always seemed to find the time for us to drop by for dinner or tea. Sometimes Alison and I slipped off to visit an exhibit. Once we stopped by when their daughter, Sarah, and her family were there. Michael was sitting in a rocking chair with his very young grandson laid out down the length of his body. He was reading *Winnie the Pooh* to Adam and they were in the middle of a crisis, as Pooh had just floated away on a balloon. We, too, floated away as quickly as possible.

Because he was such a gracious individual to us and to Baylor, each summer throughout his tenure Dean Mayne offered our students and faculty an evening tour of the Abbey after Evensong had ended and the doors had been closed to "tourists," (whom we certainly did not see ourselves to be). No one who traveled with Baylor between 1987 and 1995 will forget the sense of awe or the encounter with the sacred that we were privileged to experience during those private, sublime hours in Westminster Abbey. From the Tomb of the Unknown Warrior, to the Shrine of Edward the Confessor, from Poets' Corner to the Jerusalem Chamber, our guide, dressed in his scarlet ecclesiastical attire, gave testimony to the glory of God through Jesus of Nazareth and the serious work of the Christian church everywhere.

Many years later, Dean Mayne would articulate in prose what we could only sense at the most elementary levels as we walked with him among tombs, statues, columns, altars, and windows. Nevertheless, the experience of awe, grandeur, majesty, and history comingled within this sacred space were palpable and profound for us, in no small part because we felt the commitment of the spiritual leader of the Abbey to serving God both through the daily rhythms and prayers and through its role as a transcendent national treasure. Later, our reading of *Pray, Love, Remember* would open deeper levels of understanding of this working church and his relationship to it, for that book is among other things "a love letter to the Abbey."

At the end of each tour, he would stand at the exit from the Jerusalem Chamber and bid goodnight to each member of our group. I remember as we were shaking hands with him at the end of one of these extraordinary evenings, I remarked fervently, "I hope you are planning to write another book"— to which he replied, "Rubbish. I have written the one book in me and have said what I have to say."

But of course, fortunately for us, that was not to be the case. His second book, *This Sunrise of Wonder,* was a *tour de force* celebrating Christianity and the arts. Written during a time of retreat to the mountains of Switzerland and framed as letters to his grandchildren, Adam and Anna, these musings explore the importance of prayer, the joy of the Eucharist and the Christlikeness of God in terms that make the reader feel he or she is being granted membership in the extended family. The text interweaves Alpine flowers, weather, mountains, singing birds and walks through the countryside around and through reflections on art, poetry, and artists, such as Rilke and Van Gogh. At the conclusion of his musings, Michael speaks of the central role his wife, Alison, has played in his being able to see the visible and to sense the invisible dimensions of the world. The tribute is breath-taking. And the list of references that follows is mind boggling. I loved the book so much that as soon as I finished it, I began it again.

Jim was taken with the book, too. We bought 10 copies of *Sunrise* that summer and gave them to our closest friends. Then on our next trip to London we bought 25 more to bring home to members of our church, filling one suitcase with nothing but these treasures. Somewhere between Europe and America, however, the suitcase was lost forever in an airport transfer. The airline was apologetic and reimbursed us, but we still muse on a cold winter evening about where our trove of *Sunrise* might have ended its flight. Did some customs official open the suitcase and think the books hid contraband? If it had been easy to replace them, I might have gotten over the loss more readily, but I can still become upset about that fiasco if I dwell on the memory too long.

***

The four occasions when Michael and Alison Mayne visited Baylor should have compensated me fully for our not having been able to start the first lending library of the Dean's writings at our church. But even our campus bookstore could not seem to arrange for his books to be available for purchase when the Dean spoke on our campus. Of course, that did not diminish the effect of Michael Mayne's interactions with the students. He encountered them both through formal and informal presentations that were some of the most moving and profound we can remember. Dean Mayne's voice was magisterial; his training at BBC Radio stood him in good stead when he was asked to address fifteen-hundred freshmen at Chapel at Baylor. And the power of his presence was equally formidable. There is no question that Chapel is the toughest audience a speaker can face at our university. But when Michael Mayne, like a lion rising, spoke at that service, no creature great or small stirred in the vast hall. He asked provocative questions, told vivid stories about the work of Mother Teresa, and drew the young men and women within the wide circle of reverence, love, and respect that emanated from him wherever he spoke.

On the last occasion that he addressed faculty, students and the community here, in 1998, he was one of three guests for our prestigious Beall-Russell lectures. That October our distinguished speakers addressed standing-room-only crowds in our largest auditorium. Since Michael Mayne's presentation was the middle one, he described himself as "placed ...between the two giants of Bill Moyers and Edward Said, like some modest English muffin caught between two Big Macs." (No one ever said Reverend Mayne had no sense of humor!)

His talk was titled "The Idea of the University," and has been published by Baylor. In it he spoke vividly about the nature and purpose of a university, mused on the context at Oxford within which John Henry Newman's writings on this topic emerged, noted the tendency of modern institutions in England to drift from any theological moorings, and encouraged Baylor to remain true to both the academic and the spiritual dimensions of education. This was no "modest English muffin" speaking but an extraordinary spiritual leader who affirmed our university's mission and challenged us to be transformative in the world. He concluded his remarks this way:

> Rabbi Heschel said in his old age: "I did not ask for success: I asked for wonder." And there is a Jewish rabbinic saying that at the Final Judgment the only question God will ask of us is this: "Did you *enjoy* my world?" My ideal university would understand both those sayings, and affirm them.

When I think about the profound effect he had on our church, our university, and our community each time he and Alison visited, I find myself getting cheeky about how special and unique the community here is. Young and not so young gravitated to Dean Mayne. And I am inclined to think more Wacoans and Baylorites heard Michael speak, studied his books through our churches, and experienced his dynamic presence than any other group of Americans. (This is a qualitative, not a quantitative assessment, of course. I have absolutely no data—just a feeling—on which I base this assertion.) But I am fully reconciled to giving up our distinctive claim when *Gratitude and Grace* begins to work its magic and when other church and university groups are as deeply blessed as we in the Baptist and Episcopal fellowships in Central Texas have been by exposure to Michael Mayne's work.

***

And as the years went by, our families became more important to one another. (You can understand that the Maynes would be many splendored beings to us, but it is even now extremely hard to imagine how we might have had anything to offer them.) Nevertheless, they invited us to stay with them in the Deanery on several occasions. The first time, and every time thereafter in London and later in Salisbury, Alison and Michael set out stacks of books on each side of the bed—one for Jim and the other for me. Then when they came to stay with us in Waco, we would do the same, proffering every significant piece of American prose or poetry we thought they might not already know. Oh, how much fun those exchanges were! I realized again and again that, truly, I was the luckiest girl in the world to have such friends!

And I've been stacking books for myself and others ever since. Even to write this reflection on Michael's life and works, I felt the need to pull many of his and our shared friends from the shelves to help me find the words. These are here beside me—George Herbert, Ronald Blythe, Mary Oliver, John Clare, Gerard Manley Hopkins, John Burnsides, Francis Kilvert, T.S. Eliot, Emily Dickinson, George Steiner, Frederick Buechner, R.S. Thomas, Seamus Heaney, Czeslaw Milosz, Marilynne Robinson, and the King James translation of the Bible — to name a few.

***

Our last visit was in July of 2006 in Salisbury. I came to say goodbye, but of course I could find no words. Michael's voice was weak, but he chose to read me a poem from a new book by Billy Collins; the poem, "The Reverant" was written from the viewpoint of a dog. We laughed. He gave me a book by Victor Gollancz, *A Year of Grace*. I think I may have brought flowers. We had lunch at the pine table. Alison and I had tea in a meadow. Michael stood outside in sunlight and watched as Alison and I drove away to the train station. What I wish I could have said was:

> *Thank you for making time for me and for giving me the blue fire of Hopkins' kingfisher. I memorized it and have it now in my bones. Thank you for sharing your Salisbury Cathedral with me. Remember that morning when we were walking up to the cathedral and you told me sometimes you thought you saw it move? I never told you, but I saw it move, too. Thank you for writing your books. Jim and I hear your voice and break bread with you and Alison when we read your words about Eucharist. Thank you for having the courage and the wisdom to create a memorial at the Abbey to honor and remember the innocent victims of oppression, violence, and war. Thank you for taking me to Bemerton, where I could kneel where Herbert knelt. Thank you for sharing Alison with me. Thank you for writing Learning to Dance. It helped me learn to dance with the bees, with the cosmos, with love, and faith. Thank you for helping me learn to listen for a bird's song at dawn and to not miss a sherbet-colored sky at sunset—as Conrad said, "to see, really see." Thank you for loving the church, its imperfect but sacrificial way of testifying to Christ's love and God's kingdom. Thank you for writing about "dancing in the dark," so I could have a resource when doubt overwhelms my understanding of God or when death comes "like a hungry bear in autumn." If I could I would bring you all the health left in the world. I would fly it here at the speed of light on blue and iridescent wings.*

Michael's last words for us all were published three months later. *The Enduring Melody* makes it clear — even in facing cancer and death — this man of God had the faith to endure his last year "with gratitude for all that has been." So we know his answer when asked at the Final Judgment if he had enjoyed God's world. *Yes, and yes again.*

I close with one last remembrance of Michael's contributions to our lives. To go there, we must return to the Abbey where he affirms in *Pray, Love, Remember* the remarkable experience he had had in his years of public and private life as Dean, saying "Basically, I was me." And in the fullness of that self, Michael had had an artist paint words from Boethius around the rim of the walls, just below the ceiling, in the Abbot's Pew. He took Jim and me through his home and out a door that opened to the Abbot's Pew on several occasions. It is a space that is like a balcony within the Deanery where a Dean might look out unobserved into the beauty, stillness, mystery, and wonder of that 800 year old structure. Those words, more than any of the thousands of other phrases he honored and cherished, signify the soul competence of Michael Mayne and were affirmed in his thoughts and prayers, in his many splendid words, in his blessed way of being in the world, and always through his covenant with Christ:

To see thee is the end and the beginning,

Thou carriest me and thou dost go before,

Thou art the journey and the journey's end.

Elizabeth Vardaman
Waco, Texas

SOURCES CONSULTED

Works by Michael Mayne

Mayne, Michael. *A Year Lost and Found*. With a foreword by Gerald Priestland. London: Darton, Longman and Todd, 1987.

_____. *A Year Lost and Found*. 2007 Edition. With a foreword by Sister Frances Dominica. London: Darton, Longman and Todd, 2007.

_____. *The Enduring Melody*. With a foreword by Gerard W. Hughes, SJ. London: Darton, Longman and Todd, 2006.

_____. *Learning to Dance*. With a foreword by Dame Cicely Saunders. London: Darton, Longman and Todd, 2001.

_____. "M. E. (Chronic Fatigue Syndrome)." n. d. The Guild of St. Raphael. 24 November 2008. http://www.guild-of-st-raphael.org.uk/m_e_.htm.

_____. *Prayers for Pastoral Occasions*. London and Oxford: Mowbray, 1982.

_____. *Pray, Love, Remember*. With a foreword by Alan Bennett. London: Darton, Longman and Todd, 1998.

_____. *Something Understood: Talks on Prayer*. London: Barnard and Westwood Ltd., 1996.

_____. *This Sunrise of Wonder: Letters to my grandchildren*. With a foreword by Ronald Blythe. London: Fount, 1995.

_____. *This Sunrise of Wonder: Letters for the Journey*. New Edition. London: Darton, Longman and Todd, 2008.

_____. "The Celebration of the 950th Anniversary of the Founding of the Church of St. Mary." In *Coventry's First Cathedral:The Cathedral and Priory of St. Mary*. Papers from the 1993 Anniversary Symposium, ed. George Demidowicz. Stamford, England: Paul Watkins, 1994, 190-92.

_____. "The Idea of a University." *Beall-Russell Humanities Festival, 1998*. Waco, TX: Baylor University, 1998.

_____. Essay on *A Year Lost and Found*. n.d. Photocopied.

_____, ed. *Encounters: Exploring Christian Faith*. With an Introduction by Michael Mayne. Foreword by Robert Runcie. London: Darton, Longman, and Todd, 1986.

_____. Introduction to *Clergymen of the Church of England*, by Anthony Trollope. London: The Trollope Society, 1998, vii–xix.

_____, compiler. *The Norton Prayer Book*. London: privately printed, 1970.

_____. Review of *Embracing the Chaos: Theological Responses to AIDS*, ed. by James Woodward. *Theology* 93 (September/October 1990): 416-7.

_____. Review of *The Stranger in the Wings: Affirming Faith in a God of Surprises*, by Richard Holloway. *Theology* 98 (May/June 1995): 246-7.

_____. Review of *Doubt: The Way of Growth*, by Martin Israel. *Theology* 101 (March/April 1998): 133-4.

_____. Letter to Brendan Walsh. 21 January 2000. Photocopied.

_____. Letter to Brendan Walsh. 8 January 2001. Photocopied.

_____. Letter to Brendan Walsh. 1 April 2006. Photocopied.

_____. Letter to Brendan Walsh. 23 April 2006. Photocopied.

_____. Letter to Brendan Walsh. 18 October 2006. Photocopied.

Secondary Sources

Alexander, David. "A Very Personal Tour of the Abbey." *London Link*, Advent 1999, 16.

Amir, Dorit. "Spiritual Music Therapy: Opening Ourselves to the Mysterious Qualities of Music Therapy." 4 November 2002. Voices: A World Forum for Music Therapy. 24 November 2008. http://www.voices.no/columnist/colamir041102.html.

Baker, John Austin. *The Foolishness of God*. London: Darton, Longman and Todd, 1970.

_____. Review of *Learning to Dance*, by Michael Mayne. *The Salisbury Cathedral News*. n.d. Photocopied.

_____. Review of *This Sunrise of Wonder*, by Michael Mayne. *Times Literary Supplement*, 9 March 2007, 26.

Ballard, Richard. Review of *This Sunrise of Wonder*, by Michael Mayne. *Elizabethan Newsletter*, Election Term, 1995, 2.

Barton, John. Obituary for Michael Mayne. *The Church of England Newspaper*, 3 November 2006, 28.

Battle, Michael. *Practicing Reconciliation in a Violent World*. Harrisburg, PA: Morehouse, 2005.

_____. *Reconciliation: The Ubuntu Theology of Desmond Tutu*. Cleveland, OH: The Pilgrim Press, 1997.

Bernadin, Joseph Cardinal. *The Gift of Peace*. London: Darton, Longman and Todd, 1998.

Billsborrow, Patricia. "Travelling Down Spiritual and Theological Paths." *Methodist Recorder*, 31 January, 2002. Photocopied.

Blythe, Ronald. "Word from Wormingford." *Church Times*, 3 November, 2006, 40.

_____. "Word from Wormingford." *Church Times*, 17 November, 2006, 40.

_____. "Word from Wormingford." *Church Times*, 16 February, 2007, 40.

Brown, Rosalind. "Cantus Firmus: The Enduring Melody." Sermon preached at Durham Cathedral, 8 October 2006. Photocopied.

Brown, W. Dale. *The Book of Buechner: A Journey Through His Writings*. Louisville: Westminster John Knox Press, 2006.

Buechner, Frederick. *A Room Called Remember: Uncollected Pieces.* New York: HarperSanFrancisco, 1984.

_____. *Now and Then.* New York: HarperSanFrancisco, 1983.

_____. Personal correspondence, 15 October, 2008.

_____. *Secrets in the Dark: A Life in Sermons.* New York: HarperSanFrancisco, 2006.

_____. *Speak What We Feel (Not What We Ought to Say): Reflections on Literature and Faith.* New York: HarperSanFrancisco, 2001.

_____. *Telling Secrets.* New York: HarperSanFrancisco, 1991.

_____. *The Yellow Leaves: A Miscellany.* Louisville: Westminster John Knox Press, 2008.

Buechner, Frederick, and Michael Mayne. "1996 Bowen Conference Keynote addresses and meditations." Recorded from the 1996 Bowen Conference, 25-28 March 1996. Kanuga Conferences, 1996. Cassette.

Carey, George. "Michael Ramsey's Response to *Honest to God.*" In *Michael Ramsey as Theologian,* ed. Robin Gill and Lorna Kendall, 159 – 75. Cambridge, MA: Cowley Publications, 1995.

_____. *Why I Believe in a Personal God: The Credibility of Faith in a Doubting Culture.* Wheaton, IL: Harold Shaw Publishers, 1989.

Chittister, Joan. *The Gift of Years: Growing Older Gracefully.* New York: BlueBridge, 2008.

"City is Set to Salute Very Reverend Michael Mayne." *The Salisbury Journal,* 2 November 2006, 10.

Claypool, John R. *God the Ingenius Alchemist: Transforming Tragedy into Blessing.* Harrisburg, PA: Morehouse Publishing, 2005.

Coffin, William Sloane. *Credo.* Louisville: Westminster John Knox Press, 2004.

Conner, David J. Review of *A Year Lost and Found,* by Michael Mayne. *The Newsletter, Great St. Mary's, The University Church,* November 1987, 4.

Connor, George. *Hints and Guesses II: Selected Commentaries, 1982-1997.* Chattanooga, TN: St. Peter's Episcopal Church, 1997.

_____. *Living with the Word.* Edited, with an Introduction by Charles Thornbury. Foreword by Frederick Buechner. Chattanooga, TN: The George Connor Society, 2004.

Craig, Yvonne. Review of *Pray, Love, Remember,* by Michael Mayne. *Way of Life,* January-March 1999, 32-33.

Davies, Jeremy. "The Devil in the Deep Blue Sea." Sermon preached at Salisbury Cathedral for the All Souls' Requiem, 2 November 2006. Photocopied.

_____. "Gratitude and Grace." Sermon preached at Salisbury Cathedral for the Funeral Mass of Michael Mayne, 3 November 2006. Photocopied.

_____. Sermon preached at St. Paul's Cathedral, London, for the Annual Celebrations of St. Cecilia for the Musicians Benevolent Fund, 22 November 2006. Photocopied.

De Caussade, Jean-Pierre. *The Sacrament of the Present Moment.* With an Introduction by Richard J. Foster. Translated by Kitty Muggeridge. New York: HarperSanFancisco, 1981.

De-la-Noy, Michael. *Mervyn Stockwood: A Lonely Life.* London: Mowbray, 1996.

Dillard, Annie. *For the Time Being*. New York: Vintage Books, 1999.

_____. *Pilgrim at Tinker Creek*. New York: Perennial Classics, 1974.

_____. *Teaching a Stone to Talk: Expeditions and Encounters*. New York: HarperPerennial, 1982.

_____. *The Writing Life*. New York: HarperPerennial, 1990.

Dominica, Sister Frances. "Singer at One with His Song." *Church Times*, 30 March 2007, 25.

Donoghue, Joyce. Review of *The Enduring Melody*, by Michael Mayne. *Making Christ Known: Holy Trinity, Cuckfield, Parish Magazine*, April 2007, 17-18.

Duffy, Eamon. Sermon preached at Great St. Mary's (The University Church), Cambridge, for a Eucharist of Remembering and Thanksgiving for Michael Mayne, 22 January 2007. Photocopied.

Eaton, Peter. Review of *The Yellow Leaves: A Miscellany,* by Frederick Buechner. *The Living Church* 237 (7 December 2008): 24.

_____. "A Rich Life: The Writings of Michael Mayne." *The Living Church* 234 (6 May 2007): 18-19.

Edmonds-Seal, John. Review of *A Year Lost and Found*, by Michael Mayne. *Oxford Diocesan Magazine*, March 1988, 19.

Etchells, Ruth. Review of *This Sunrise of Wonder*, by Michael Mayne. *Theology* 99 (March/April 1996): 167-68.

Garton, John. Review of *This Sunrise of Wonder*, by Michael Mayne. *Ripon College Cuddesdon Newsletter*, 1996, 24.

Gomes, Peter J. *The Good Book: Reading the Bible with Mind and Heart*. New York: William Morrow and Company, Inc., 1996.

Graham, Ysenda Maxton. Review of *Pray, Love, Remember*. *Newsletter of St. Paul's Knightsbridge*, February 1999, 7-8.

Gray, Donald. Obituary for Michael Mayne. *Church Times*, 27 October 2006, 27.

Green, Bernard. "Westminster's Dean Takes Spiritual Stock." *Catholic Herald*, 10 March 1995, 6.

Gulliford, William. "Good Friday Sermon 2007." St. Dunstan In-the-West. 21 November 2008. http://www.stdunstaninthewest.org/Page%2010%20%Friday%20Sermon%20200…

Hall, Sean E. Review of *Encounters: Exploring Christian Faith*, ed. by Michael Mayne. *Clergy Review* 71 (August 1986): 311.

Hallock, Daniel. *Six Months to Live: Learning from a Young Man with Cancer*. Farmington, PA: The Plough Publishing House, 2001.

Harries, Richard. *The Real God: A Response to Anthony Freeman's God in Us*. London: Mowbray, 1994.

Harvey, Anthony. Obituary for Michael Mayne *The Independent on Sunday*, 28 October 2006. http://news.independent.co.uk/people/obituaries/article1935910.ece

_____. Obituary for Michael Mayne. *The Tablet*, 4 November 2006, 40.

_____. Personal correspondence, 19 October 2008.

_____. Personal correspondence, 22 October 2008.

Heschel, Abraham Joshua. *I Asked for Wonder: A Spiritual Anthology*. Edited, with an Introduction by Samuel H. Dresner. New York: The Crossroad Publishing Company, 1983.

Hibbert, Barrie. "The Bottom Line." Sermon preached at Flinders Street Baptist Church, Adelaide, Australia, 26 November 2006. Photocopied.

Hill, Susan. "Michael Mayne. . . Good Man, Good Priest, Good Friend." 3 November 2006. Susan Hill's Blog. 24 June 2007. http://blog.susan-hill.com/blog/_archives/2006/11/3/2471667.html

Hopkins, Hugh Evan. *Charles Simeon of Cambridge.* Grand Rapids: William B. Eerdmans Publishing Company, 1977.

House, Christopher. "A Song That Went on to the End." *Daily Telegraph,* 28 October 2006, 29.

Hoyle, David M. "Mere's Sermon." *Letter of the Corpus Association,* Corpus Christi College, Cambridge, Michaelmas 2007, 22-28.

Hume, Basil. The *Mystery of the Cross.* Brewster, MA: Paraclete Press, 1998.

_____. The *Mystery of the Incarnation.* London: Darton, Longman and Todd, 1999.

_____. The *Mystery of Love.* London: Darton, Longman and Todd, 2000.

James, Eric. *A Life of Bishop John A. T. Robinson: Scholar, Pastor, Prophet.* Grand Rapids: William B. Eerdmans Publishing Company, 1987.

Kavanaugh, P. J. "Strange Meeting." Review of *This Sunrise of Wonder,* by Michael Mayne. *The Oldie,* March 1995, 49.

Keen, Sam. *Learning to Fly: Reflections on Fear, Trust, and the Joy of Letting Go.* New York: Broadway Books, 1999.

Kefford, Paul. Review of *Pray, Love, Remember,* by Michael Mayne. *Oremus,* February 1999, 12.

Lamott, Anne. *Bird by Bird: Some Instructions on Writing and Life.* New York: Anchor Books, 1994.

_____. *Traveling Mercies: Some Thoughts on Faith.* New York: Pantheon Books, 1999.

"Lives Remembered." Obituary for Michael Mayne. *The Times,* 14 November 2006.

Long, Anne. Review of *The Enduring Melody,* by Michael Mayne. *The Pastoral Review* 4 (May/June 2008): 94.

Lywood, Wendy. "Rediscovering My Priesthood." *In Befriending Life: Encounters with Henri Nouwen,* ed. Beth Porter, with Susan M. Brown and Philip Coulter, 232 – 37. New York: Image Books, 2001.

McAllister, Margaret. "What I'm Reading." *Church Times,* 28 September 2007, 22.

McCrum, Robert. "Hope Lives on in 'Cancer Country.'" *The Observer,* 17 September 2006.

McFarlane, Graham. Review of *This Sunrise of Wonder,* by Michael Mayne. *Third Way,* March 1995, 30.

McGrath, Alister. *What Was God Doing on the Cross?* Grand Rapids: Zondervan Publishing House, 1992.

McKinnon, Cleodie. Review of *Learning to Dance,* by Michael Mayne. 25 November 2001. Thegoodbookstall.org.uk. 21 May 2008. http://www.thegoodbookstall.org.uk/review/0232524343/michael-mayne/learning-to-dance/.

McNamara, James. *The Power of Compassion: Innocence and Powerlessness as Adversaries of the Spiritual Life.* Ramsey, NJ: Paulist Press, 1983.

Magill, Lucanne. "Music Therapy in Spirituality." 2002. Music Therapy World. 21November 2008. http://www.musictherapyworld.de/modules/mmmagizine/showarticle .php

Marshall, Michael. "Recovering a Sense of Wonder of Being Human." *The Church of England Newspaper*, 31 March 1995, 10.

Martin, Alan A. Obituary for Michael Mayne. *Edward Thomas Fellowship Newsletter*, 2007, 3-4.

Mathis, Rick. *Finding a Grace-Filled Life*. New York: Paulist Press, 2008.

Mercer, Rick. "Time With a Well-Stocked Mind." *Church Times*, 22 March 2002, 17.

Montefiore, Hugh. *Credible Christianity: The Gospel in Contemporary Society*. Grand Rapids: William B. Eerdmans Publishing Company, 1993.

Moore, Thomas. *Dark Nights of the Soul: A Guide to Finding Your Way Through Life's Ordeals*. New York: Gotham Books, 2004.

Morgan, Barry. Personal correspondence. 20 March 2008.

Neuhaus, Richard John. *As I Lay Dying: Meditations Upon Returning*. New York: Basic Books, 2002.

Nouwen, Henri J. M. *Beloved: Henri Nouwen in Conversation*. Edited by Philip Roderick. Grand Rapids: William B. Eerdmans Publishing Company, 2007.

_____. *The Inner Voice of Love: A Journey Through Anguish to Freedom*. New York: Image Books, 1996.

_____. *Jesus & Mary: Finding Our Sacred Center*. Cincinnati: St. Anthony Messenger Press, 1993.

_____. *Life of the Beloved: Spiritual Living in a Secular World*. New York: Crossroad, 1992.

_____. *The Road to Daybreak: A Spiritual Journey*. New York: Image Books, 1990.

_____. *Turn My Mourning into Dancing: Moving Through Hard Times with Hope*, ed. Timothy Jones. Nashville: W. Publishing Group, 2001.

_____. *The Wounded Healer: Ministry in Contemporary Society*. New York: Image Books, 1979.

Oakley, Mark. *The Collage of God*. London: Darton, Longman and Todd, 2001.

Obituary for Michael Mayne. *The Daily Telegraph*, 24 October 2006, 27.

Obituary for Michael Mayne. *Letter of the Corpus Association*. Cambridge: Corpus Christi College, 2007.

Obituary for Michael Mayne. *The Times*, 25 October 2006, 68.

Obituary for Michael Mayne. Westminster Abbey. http://www.westminster-abbey.org/article.htm?article=20061022_mayne.inc.

O'Donohue, John. *Eternal Echoes: Exploring Our Yearning to Belong*. New York: Cliff Street Books, 1999.

O'Driscoll, Herbert. "Thank You." *Anglican Fellowship of Prayer Canada Newsletter*. Spring 2008: 1-2.

O'Laughlin, Michael. *God's Beloved: A Spiritual Biography of Henri Nouwen*. Maryknoll, NY: Orbis Books, 2004.

O'Leary, Daniel. "Autumn Song." *The Tablet*, 13 October 2007, 8.

Pausch, Randy, and Jeffrey Zaslow. *The Last Lecture*. London: Hodder & Stoughton, 2008.

Paterson, Marie. Review of *Pray, Love, Remember*. by Michael Mayne. *The Reader*. Autumn 1999, 113.

Perry, Michael. "Not So Much a Retreat, More of a Challenge." Review of *Pray, Love, Remember*, by Michael Mayne. *Church Times*, 29 January 1999, 14-15.

Pirouet, Louise, and Janet Ferguson. Obituary for Michael Mayne. *Majestas: The Magazine of Great St. Mary's, The University Church, Cambridge*, February 2007, 1-2.

Quindlen, Anna. *A Short Guide to a Happy Life*. New York: Random House, 2000.

Review of *A Year Lost and Found*, by Michael Mayne. *Methodist Recorder*, 10 December 1987, 20.

Review of *A Year Lost and Found*, by Michael Mayne. *Way of Life*, July-September 1994, 79.

Review of *Learning to Dance*, by Michael Mayne. *England on Sunday*, 14 December 2001, 22.

Review of *Learning to Dance*, by Michael Mayne. *Parish News*, February 2002, 6. Photocopied.

Review of *Pray, Love, Remember*, by Michael Mayne. *Church Times*, 29 January 1999.

Review of *Pray, Love, Remember*, by Michael Mayne. *The Westminster Abbey Chorister* 3 (Winter 1998/9): 44-46.

Robinson, John A. T. *Honest to God*. Philadelphia: Westminster Press, 1963.

Roose-Evans, James. "Felt on the Pulse." *The Tablet*, 25 February 1995, 261.

_____. "Heroic Last Testament." *The Tablet*, 4 November 2006, 24.

_____. "Meditations in Stones." *The Tablet*, 30 January 1999, 148.

Rose, Gillian. *Love's Work: A Reckoning with Life*. New York: Schocken Books, 1995.

Sacks, Jonathan. "Love Can Teach Us to Listen to Our Enduring Melodies." *The Times*, 2 February 2008, 73.

Sagovsky, Nicholas. "A Year Lost and Found." Sermon preached at Westminster Abbey, 5 November 2006. Photocopied.

_____. "Learning to Dance." Sermon preached at Westminster Abbey, 26 November 2006. Photocopied.

_____. "Michael Mayne." Sermon preached at Westminster Abbey for the Memorial Service for Michael Mayne, 1 February 2007. Photocopied.

_____. "Pray, Love, Remember." Sermon preached at Westminster Abbey, 19 November 2006. Photocopied.

_____. "This Sunrise of Wonder." Sermon preached at Westminster Abbey, 12 November 2006. Photocopied.

Schmidt, Richard H. *Glorious Companions: Five Centuries of Anglican Spirituality*. Grand Rapids: William B. Eerdmans Publishing Company, 2003.

Scott, David. Review of *Learning to Dance*, by Michael Mayne. *The Franciscan* 15 (May 2003): 14.

Silf, Margaret. "Rhythm of Life." *The Tablet*, 18 May 2002, 25.

Smith, Donald P. *Empowering Ministry: Ways to Grow in Effectiveness.* Louisville: Westminster John Knox Press, 1996.

Sorréll, Stephanie. Review of *A Year Lost and Found*, by Michael Mayne. *The Review*, November/December 1994, 187.

Stack, George. "Finding God in Cancer." Sermon preached at the Cardinal Vaughan School, London, 14 October 2007. Photocopied.

Starkey, Mike. "Fireside Chat." *Christian Herald*, 9 February 2002, 7.

Stock, Victor. "Finding Your Still Centre." *Church Times*, 1 November 2002, 18.

Symon, Roger. Review of *The Enduring Melody*, by Michael Mayne. *OKS Offcuts*, 19 January 2007, 1-7.

Taylor, Barbara Brown. *Leaving Church: A Memoir of Faith.* New York: HarperSanFrancisco, 2006.

Thrower, Debbie. "What I'm Reading." Review of *Pray, Love, Remember*, by Michael Mayne. *Church Times*, 14 October 2005, 24.

Tutu, Desmond. *No Future Without Forgiveness.* New York: Image Books, 1999.

Vardaman, Elizabeth. "Meditation Thirty." In *Advent, Christmas & Epiphany Devotionals 2007,* ed. by Carol Low. Waco, TX: The Worship Council of Seventh and James Baptist Church, 2007.

_____. Personal Correspondence. 30 December 2008.

Vickers, Salley. Review of *The Enduring Melody*, by Michael Mayne. *The Times*, 29 July 2006. Photocopied.

Waller, John. Personal correspondence. 8 December 2008.

Walsh, Brendan. Letter to Michael Mayne. 19 May 2006. Photocopied.

_____. Letter to Alison Mayne, Mark Mayne, and Sarah Mayne Tyndall. 23 October 2006. Photocopied.

"What You Thought of *Learning to Dance* by Michael Mayne." *Church Times,* 6 December 2002, 17.

Williams, Rowan. *Anglican Identities.* Cambridge, MA: Cowley Publications, 2003.

_____. *Christ on Trial: How the Gospel Unsettles Our Judgement.* Grand Rapids: William B. Eerdmans Publishing Company, 2000.

_____. Personal correspondence. 13 November 2007.

_____. *Tokens of Trust: An Introduction to Christian Beliefs.* Louisville: Westminster John Knox Press, 2007.

_____. *Where God Happens: Discovering Christ in One Another.* Boston: New Seeds, 2005.

Wilson, A. N. "Marvels of Faith." *Evening Standard,* 30 January 1995, 24.

Yancey, Philip. *Soul Survivor: How Thirteen Unlikely Mentors Helped My Faith Survive The Church.* Colorado Springs, CO: Waterbrook Press, 2001.

Index

About the Author

Joel W. Huffstetler is Rector of St. Luke's Episcopal Church in Cleveland, Tennessee. Previously he served as Rector of St. Andrew's Episcopal Church in Canton, North Carolina, and as Assistant to the Rector of St. Paul's Episcopal Church in Chattanooga, Tennessee. He is a graduate (*summa cum laude*) of Elon College, and of The School of Theology, The University of the South (Sewanee), earning his Master of Divinity degree in 1990, Doctor of Ministry in 2006, and Master of Sacred Theology in 2009. He also studied at Candler School of Theology, Emory University. He is the author of *Boundless Love: The Parable of the Prodigal Son and Reconciliation* (University Press of America, 2008) as well as two other books and numerous articles and reviews. He and his wife Debbie live in Cleveland, Tennessee.